Optimizing Hadoop for MapReduce

Learn how to configure your Hadoop cluster to run optimal MapReduce jobs

Khaled Tannir

[PACKT] open source ✳

PUBLISHING

community experience distilled

BIRMINGHAM - MUMBAI

Optimizing Hadoop for MapReduce

First published: February 2014

Production Reference: 1140214

Published by Packt Publishing Ltd.
Livery Place
35 Livery Street
Birmingham B3 2PB, UK.

ISBN 978-1-78328-565-5

www.packtpub.com

Cover Image by Khaled Tannir (contact@khaledtannir.net)

Credits

Author
Khaled Tannir

Reviewers
Włodzimierz Bzyl
Craig Henderson
Mark Kerzner

Acquisition Editor
Joanne Fitzpatrick

Commissioning Editor
Manasi Pandire

Technical Editors
Mario D'Souza
Rosmy George
Pramod Kumavat
Arwa Manasawala
Adrian Raposo

Copy Editors
Kirti Pai
Laxmi Subramanian

Project Coordinator
Aboli Ambardekar

Proofreaders
Simran Bhogal
Ameesha Green

Indexer
Rekha Nair

Graphics
Yuvraj Mannari

Production Coordinators
Manu Joseph
Alwin Roy

Cover Work
Alwin Roy

About the Author

Khaled Tannir has been working with computers since 1980. He began programming with the legendary Sinclair Zx81 and later with Commodore home computer products (Vic 20, Commodore 64, Commodore 128D, and Amiga 500).

He has a Bachelor's degree in Electronics, a Master's degree in System Information Architectures, in which he graduated with a professional thesis, and completed his education with a Master of Research degree.

He is a Microsoft Certified Solution Developer (MCSD) and has more than 20 years of technical experience leading the development and implementation of software solutions and giving technical presentations. He now works as an independent IT consultant and has worked as an infrastructure engineer, senior developer, and enterprise/solution architect for many companies in France and Canada.

With significant experience in Microsoft .Net, Microsoft Server Systems, and Oracle Java technologies, he has extensive skills in online/offline applications design, system conversions, and multilingual applications in both domains: Internet and Desktops.

He is always researching new technologies, learning about them, and looking for new adventures in France, North America, and the Middle-east. He owns an IT and electronics laboratory with many servers, monitors, open electronic boards such as Arduino, Netduino, RaspBerry Pi, and .Net Gadgeteer, and some smartphone devices based on Windows Phone, Android, and iOS operating systems.

In 2012, he contributed to the EGC 2012 (International Complex Data Mining forum at Bordeaux University, France) and presented, in a workshop session, his work on "how to optimize data distribution in a cloud computing environment". This work aims to define an approach to optimize the use of data mining algorithms such as k-means and Apriori in a cloud computing environment.

He is the author of *RavenDB 2.x Beginner's Guide, Packt Publishing*.

He aims to get a PhD in Cloud Computing and Big Data and wants to learn more and more about these technologies.

He enjoys taking landscape and night time photos, travelling, playing video games, creating funny electronic gadgets with Arduino/.Net Gadgeteer, and of course, spending time with his wife and family.

You can reach him at contact@khaledtannir.net.

Acknowledgments

All praise is due to Allah, the Lord of the Worlds. First, I must thank Allah for giving me the ability to think and write.

Next, I would like to thank my wife, Laila, for her big support, encouragement, and patience throughout this project. Also, I would like to thank my family in Canada and Lebanon for their support during the writing of this book.

I would like to thank everyone at Packt Publishing for their help and guidance, and for giving me the opportunity to share my experience and knowledge in technology with others in the Hadoop and MapReduce community.

Thank you as well to the technical reviewers, who provided great feedback to ensure that every tiny technical detail was accurate and rich in content.

About the Reviewers

Włodzimierz Bzyl works at the University of Gdańsk, Poland. His current interests include web-related technologies and NoSQL databases. He has a passion for new technologies and introduces his students to them. He enjoys contributing to open source software and spending time trekking in the Tatra mountains.

Craig Henderson graduated in 1995 with a degree in Computing for Real-time Systems and has spent his career working on large-scale data processing and distributed systems. He is the author of an open source C++ MapReduce library for single server application scalability, which is available at `https://github.com/cdmh/mapreduce`, and he currently researches image and video processing techniques for person identification.

Mark Kerzner holds degrees in Law, Mathematics, and Computer Science. He has been designing software for many years and Hadoop-based systems since 2008. He is the President of SHMsoft, a provider of Hadoop applications for various verticals, a co-founder of the Hadoop Illuminated training and consulting, and also the co-author of the open source book, *Hadoop Illuminated*. He has also authored and co-authored other books and patents.

I would like to acknowledge the help of my colleagues, in particular Sujee Maniyam, and last but not least, my multitalented family.

www.PacktPub.com

Support files, eBooks, discount offers and more

You might want to visit www.PacktPub.com for support files and downloads related to your book.

Did you know that Packt offers eBook versions of every book published, with PDF and ePub files available? You can upgrade to the eBook version at www.PacktPub.com and as a print book customer, you are entitled to a discount on the eBook copy. Get in touch with us at service@packtpub.com for more details.

At www.PacktPub.com, you can also read a collection of free technical articles, sign up for a range of free newsletters and receive exclusive discounts and offers on Packt books and eBooks.

http://PacktLib.PacktPub.com

Do you need instant solutions to your IT questions? PacktLib is Packt's online digital book library. Here, you can access, read and search across Packt's entire library of books.

Why Subscribe?

- Fully searchable across every book published by Packt
- Copy and paste, print and bookmark content
- On demand and accessible via web browser

Free Access for Packt account holders

If you have an account with Packt at www.PacktPub.com, you can use this to access PacktLib today and view nine entirely free books. Simply use your login credentials for immediate access.

Table of Contents

Preface

MapReduce is an important parallel processing model for large-scale, data-intensive applications such as data mining and web indexing. Hadoop, an open source implementation of MapReduce, is widely applied to support cluster computing jobs that require low response time.

Most of the MapReduce programs are written for data analysis and they usually take a long time to finish. Many companies are embracing Hadoop for advanced data analytics over large datasets that require time completion guarantees. Efficiency, especially the I/O costs of MapReduce, still needs to be addressed for successful implications. The experience shows that a misconfigured Hadoop cluster can noticeably reduce and significantly downgrade the performance of MapReduce jobs.

In this book, we address the MapReduce optimization problem, how to identify shortcomings, and what to do to get using all of the Hadoop cluster's resources to process input data optimally. This book starts off with an introduction to MapReduce to learn how it works internally, and discusses the factors that can affect its performance. Then it moves forward to investigate Hadoop metrics and performance tools, and identifies resource weaknesses such as CPU contention, memory usage, massive I/O storage, and network traffic.

This book will teach you, in a step-by-step manner based on real-world experience, how to eliminate your job bottlenecks and fully optimize your MapReduce jobs in a production environment. Also, you will learn to calculate the right number of cluster nodes to process your data, to define the right number of mapper and reducer tasks based on your hardware resources, and how to optimize mapper and reducer task performances using compression technique and combiners.

Finally, you will learn the best practices and recommendations to tune your Hadoop cluster and learn what a MapReduce template class looks like.

What this book covers

Chapter 1, Understanding Hadoop MapReduce, explains how MapReduce works internally and the factors that affect MapReduce performance.

Chapter 2, An Overview of the Hadoop Parameters, introduces Hadoop configuration files and MapReduce performance-related parameters. It also explains Hadoop metrics and several performance monitoring tools that you can use to monitor Hadoop MapReduce activities.

Chapter 3, Detecting System Bottlenecks, explores Hadoop MapReduce performance tuning cycle and explains how to create a performance baseline. Then you will learn to identify resource bottlenecks and weaknesses based on Hadoop counters.

Chapter 4, Identifying Resource Weaknesses, explains how to check the Hadoop cluster's health and identify CPU and memory usage, massive I/O storage, and network traffic. Also, you will learn how to scale correctly when configuring your Hadoop cluster.

Chapter 5, Enhancing Map and Reduce Tasks, shows you how to enhance map and reduce task execution. You will learn the impact of block size, how to reduce spilling records, determine map and reduce throughput, and tune MapReduce configuration parameters.

Chapter 6, Optimizing MapReduce Tasks, explains when you need to use combiners and compression techniques to optimize map and reduce tasks and introduces several techniques to optimize your application code.

Chapter 7, Best Practices and Recommendations, introduces miscellaneous hardware and software checklists, recommendations, and tuning properties in order to use your Hadoop cluster optimally.

What you need for this book

Apache Hadoop framework (http://hadoop.apache.org/) with access to a computer running Hadoop on a Linux operating system.

Who this book is for

If you are an experienced MapReduce user or developer, this book will be great for you. The book can also be a very helpful guide if you are a MapReduce beginner or user who wants to try new things and learn techniques to optimize your applications. Knowledge of creating a MapReduce application is not required, but will help you to grasp some of the concepts quicker and become more familiar with the snippets of MapReduce class template code.

Conventions

In this book, you will find a number of styles of text that distinguish between different kinds of information. Here are some examples of these styles, and an explanation of their meaning.

Code words in text, database table names, folder names, filenames, file extensions, pathnames, dummy URLs, user input, and Twitter handles are shown as follows: "We can include other contexts through the use of the `include` directive."

A block of code is set as follows:

```
[default]
exten => s,1,Dial(Zap/1|30)
exten => s,2,Voicemail(u100)
exten => s,102,Voicemail(b100)
exten => i,1,Voicemail(s0)
```

When we wish to draw your attention to a particular part of a code block, the relevant lines or items are set in bold:

```
[default]
exten => s,1,Dial(Zap/1|30)
exten => s,2,Voicemail(u100)
exten => s,102,Voicemail(b100)
exten => i,1,Voicemail(s0)
```

Any command-line input or output is written as follows:

```
# cp /usr/src/asterisk-addons/configs/cdr_mysql.conf.sample
    /etc/asterisk/cdr_mysql.conf
```

New terms and **important words** are shown in bold. Words that you see on the screen, for example, in menus or dialog boxes appear in the text like this: "clicking on the **Next** button moves you to the next screen."

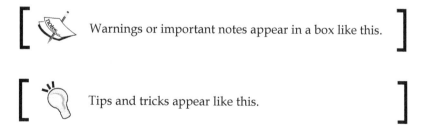

Warnings or important notes appear in a box like this.

Tips and tricks appear like this.

Reader feedback

Feedback from our readers is always welcome. Let us know what you think about this book—what you liked or may have disliked. Reader feedback is important for us to develop titles that you really get the most out of.

To send us general feedback, simply send an e-mail to feedback@packtpub.com, and mention the book title via the subject of your message.

If there is a topic that you have expertise in and you are interested in either writing or contributing to a book, see our author guide on www.packtpub.com/authors.

Customer support

Now that you are the proud owner of a Packt book, we have a number of things to help you to get the most from your purchase.

Errata

Although we have taken every care to ensure the accuracy of our content, mistakes do happen. If you find a mistake in one of our books—maybe a mistake in the text or the code—we would be grateful if you would report this to us. By doing so, you can save other readers from frustration and help us improve subsequent versions of this book. If you find any errata, please report them by visiting http://www.packtpub.com/submit-errata, selecting your book, clicking on the **errata submission form** link, and entering the details of your errata. Once your errata are verified, your submission will be accepted and the errata will be uploaded on our website, or added to any list of existing errata, under the Errata section of that title. Any existing errata can be viewed by selecting your title from http://www.packtpub.com/support.

Piracy

Piracy of copyright material on the Internet is an ongoing problem across all media. At Packt, we take the protection of our copyright and licenses very seriously. If you come across any illegal copies of our works, in any form, on the Internet, please provide us with the location address or website name immediately so that we can pursue a remedy.

Please contact us at copyright@packtpub.com with a link to the suspected pirated material.

We appreciate your help in protecting our authors, and our ability to bring you valuable content.

Questions

You can contact us at questions@packtpub.com if you are having a problem with any aspect of the book, and we will do our best to address it.

1
Understanding Hadoop MapReduce

MapReduce, the popular data-intensive distributed computing model is emerging as an important programming model for large-scale data-parallel applications such as web indexing, data mining, and scientific simulation.

Hadoop is the most popular open source Java implementation of the Google's MapReduce programming model. It is already being used for large-scale data analysis tasks by many companies and is often used for jobs where low response time is critical.

Before going deep into MapReduce programming and Hadoop performance tuning, we will review the MapReduce model basics and learn about factors that affect Hadoop's performance.

In this chapter, we will cover the following:

- The MapReduce model
- An overview of Hadoop MapReduce
- How MapReduce works internally
- Factors that affect MapReduce performance

The MapReduce model

MapReduce is a programming model designed for processing unstructured data by large clusters of commodity hardware and generating large datasets. It is capable of processing many terabytes of data on thousands of computing nodes in a cluster, handling failures, duplicating tasks, and aggregating results.

The MapReduce model is simple to understand. It was designed in the early 2000s by the engineers at Google Research (http://research.google.com/archive/mapreduce.html). It consists of two functions, a map function and a reduce function that can be executed in parallel on multiple machines.

To use MapReduce, the programmer writes a user-defined map function and a user-defined reduce function that expresses their desired computation. The map function reads a key/value pair, applies the user specific code, and produces results called intermediate results. Then, these intermediate results are aggregated by the reduce user-specific code that outputs the final results.

Input to a MapReduce application is organized in the records as per the input specification that will yield key/value pairs, each of which is a <k1, v1> pair.

Therefore, the MapReduce process consists of two main phases:

- map(): The user-defined map function is applied to all input records one by one, and for each record it outputs a list of zero or more intermediate key/value pairs, that is, <k2, v2> records. Then all <k2, v2> records are collected and reorganized so that records with the same keys (k2) are put together into a <k2, list(v2)> record.

- reduce(): The user-defined reduce function is called once for each distinct key in the map output, <k2, list(v2)> records, and for each record the reduce function outputs zero or more <k2, v3> pairs. All <k2, v3> pairs together coalesce into the final result.

The signatures of the map and reduce functions are as follows:
- map(<k1, v1>)   list(<k2, v2>)
- reduce(<k2, list(v2)>)   <k2, v3>

The MapReduce programming model is designed to be independent of storage systems. MapReduce reads key/value pairs from the underlying storage system through a reader. The reader retrieves each record from the storage system and wraps the record into a key/value pair for further processing. Users can add support for a new storage system by implementing a corresponding reader. This storage-independent design is considered to be beneficial for heterogeneous systems since it enables MapReduce to analyze data stored in different storage systems.

To understand the MapReduce programming model, let's assume you want to count the number of occurrences of each word in a given input file. Translated into a MapReduce job, the word-count job is defined by the following steps:

1. The input data is split into records.

2. Map functions process these records and produce key/value pairs for each word.

3. All key/value pairs that are output by the map function are merged together, grouped by a key, and sorted.

4. The intermediate results are transmitted to the reduce function, which will produce the final output.

The overall steps of this MapReduce application are represented in the following diagram:

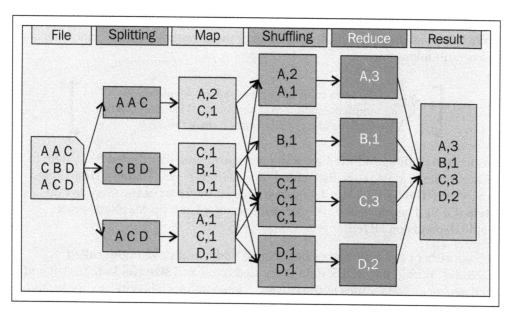

While aggregating key/value pairs, a massive amount of I/O and network traffic I/O can be observed. To reduce the amount of network traffic required between the map and reduce steps, the programmer can optionally perform a map-side pre-aggregation by supplying a **Combiner** function. Combiner functions are similar to the reduce function, except that they are not passed all the values for a given key; instead, a Combiner function emits an output value that summarizes the input values it was passed.

An overview of Hadoop MapReduce

Hadoop is the most popular open source Java implementation of the MapReduce programming model proposed by Google. There are many other implementations of MapReduce (such as Sphere, Starfish, Riak , and so on), which implement all the features described in the Google documentation or only a subset of these features.

Hadoop consists of distributed data storage engine and MapReduce execution engine. It has been successfully used for processing highly distributable problems across a large amount of datasets using a large number of nodes. These nodes collectively form a **Hadoop cluster**, which in turn consists of a single master node called **JobTracker**, and multiple worker (or slave) nodes; each worker node is called a **TaskTracker**. In this framework, a user program is called a job and is divided into two steps: map and reduce.

Like in the MapReduce programing model, the user has to only define the map and reduce functions when using the Hadoop MapReduce implementation. The Hadoop MapReduce system automatically parallelizes the execution of these functions and ensures fault tolerance.

 To learn more about the Hadoop MapReduce implementation, you can browse Hadoop's official website at http://hadoop.apache.org/.

Basically, the Hadoop MapReduce framework utilizes a distributed filesystem to read and write its data. This distributed filesystem is called **Hadoop Distributed File System** (**HDFS**), which is the open source counterpart of the **Google File System** (**GFS**). Therefore, the I/O performance of a Hadoop MapReduce job strongly depends on HDFS.

HDFS consists of a master node called **NameNode**, and slave nodes called **DataNodes**. Within the HDFS, data is divided into fixed-size blocks (chunks) and spread across all DataNodes in the cluster. Each data block is typically replicated with two replicas: one placed within the same rack and the other placed outside it. NameNode keeps track of which DataNodes hold replicas of which block.

Hadoop MapReduce internals

The MapReduce programing model can be used to process many large-scale data problems using one or more steps. Also, it can be efficiently implemented to support problems that deal with large amount of data using a large number of machines. In a Big Data context, the size of data processed may be so large that the data cannot be stored on a single machine.

In a typical Hadoop MapReduce framework, data is divided into blocks and distributed across many nodes in a cluster and the MapReduce framework takes advantage of data locality by shipping computation to data rather than moving data to where it is processed. Most input data blocks for MapReduce applications are located on the local node, so they can be loaded very fast, and reading multiple blocks can be done on multiple nodes in parallel. Therefore, MapReduce can achieve very high aggregate I/O bandwidth and data processing rate.

To launch a MapReduce job, Hadoop creates an instance of the MapReduce application and submits the job to the JobTracker. Then, the job is divided into map tasks (also called mappers) and reduce tasks (also called reducers).

When Hadoop launches a MapReduce job, it splits the input dataset into even-sized data blocks and uses a heartbeat protocol to assign a task. Each data block is then scheduled to one TaskTracker node and is processed by a map task.

Each task is executed on an available slot in a worker node, which is configured with a fixed number of map slots, and another fixed number of reduce slots. If all available slots are occupied, pending tasks must wait until some slots are freed up.

The TaskTracker node periodically sends its state to the JobTracker. When the TaskTracker node is idle, the JobTracker node assigns new tasks to it. The JobTracker node takes data locality into account when it disseminates data blocks. It always tries to assign a local data block to a TaskTracker node. If the attempt fails, the JobTracker node will assign a rack-local or random data block to the TaskTracker node instead.

When all map functions complete execution, the runtime system groups all intermediate pairs and launches a set of reduce tasks to produce the final results. It moves execution from the shuffle phase into the reduce phase. In this final reduce phase, the `reduce` function is called to process the intermediate data and write the final output.

Users often use terms with different granularities to specify Hadoop map and reduce tasks, subtasks, phases, and subphases. While the map task consists of two subtasks: map and merge, the reduce task consists of just one task. However, the shuffle and sort happen first and are done by the system. Each subtask in turn gets divided into many subphases such as read-map, spill, merge, copy-map, and reduce-write.

Factors affecting the performance of MapReduce

The processing time of input data with MapReduce may be affected by many factors. One of these factors is the algorithm you use while implementing your `map` and `reduce` functions. Other external factors may also affect the MapReduce performance. Based on our experience and observation, the following are the major factors that may affect MapReduce performance:

- Hardware (or resources) such as CPU clock, disk I/O, network bandwidth, and memory size.

- The underlying storage system.

- Data size for input data, shuffle data, and output data, which are closely correlated with the runtime of a job.

- Job algorithms (or program) such as map, reduce, partition, combine, and compress. Some algorithms may be hard to conceptualize in MapReduce, or may be inefficient to express in terms of MapReduce.

While running a map task, intermediate output of the shuffle subtasks is stored in a memory buffer to reduce disk I/O. However, since the size of this output may exceed that of the memory buffer and such an overflow may occur, the spill subphase is needed to flush the data into a local filesystem. This subphase may affect the MapReduce performance and is often implemented using multithreading to maximize the utility of disk I/O and to reduce the runtime of jobs.

The MapReduce programming model enables users to specify data transformation logic using their own `map` and `reduce` functions. The model does not specify how intermediate pairs produced by map functions are grouped for reduce functions to process. Therefore, the **merge-sort** algorithm is employed as the default grouping algorithm. However, the merge-sort algorithm is not always the most efficient algorithm, especially for analytical tasks, such as aggregation and equal-join, which do not care about the order of intermediate keys.

In the MapReduce programming model, grouping/partitioning is a *serial* task! This means the framework needs to wait for all map tasks to complete before any reduce tasks can be run.

To learn more about the merge-sort algorithm, refer to the URL http://en.wikipedia.org/wiki/Merge_sort.

The MapReduce performance is based on the runtime of both `map` and `reduce`. This is because parameters such as the number of nodes in a cluster or the number of slots in a node are unmodifiable in a typical environment.

Other factors that may potentially affect the performance of MapReduce are:

- **The I/O mode**: This is the way to retrieve data from the storage system. There are two modes to read data from the underlying storage system:

    ○ **Direct I/O**: This is used to read directly from the local disk cache to memory through hardware controllers; therefore, no inter-process communication costs are required.

    ○ **Streaming I/O**: This allows you to read data from another running process (typically the storage system process) through certain inter-process communication schemes such as TCP/IP and JDBC.

 To enhance performance, using direct I/O may be more efficient than streaming I/O.

- **Input data parsing**: This is the conversion process from raw data into the key/value pairs when data is retrieved from the storage system. The data parsing process aims to decode raw data from its native format and transform it into data objects that can be processed by a programming language such as Java.

    Input data can be decoded to (Java or other) objects so that the content can be altered after an instance is created, typically when you use a reference to an instance of the object (these objects are called **mutable** objects) or to objects where the content cannot be altered after it is created (called **immutable** objects). In the case of a million records, the immutable decoding process is significantly slower than the mutable decoding process as it may produce a huge number of immutable objects. Therefore, this can lead to poor performance of the system.

- **Input data storage**: The underlining storage system must ensure a high speed access and data availability (such as HDFS, and HBase) when data is retrieved by MapReduce to be processed. If you choose to use a storage filesystem other than those recommended to be used with MapReduce, the access to the input data may potentially affect MapReduce performance.

When using the Hadoop framework, many factors may affect the overall system performance and the runtime of a job. These factors may be part of the Hadoop MapReduce engine or may be external to it.

The Hadoop configuration parameters usually indicate how many tasks can run concurrently and determine the runtime of a job since other factors are not modifiable after the Hadoop cluster is set up and the job starts the execution. A misconfigured Hadoop framework may underutilize the cluster resources and therefore impact the MapReduce job performance. This is due to the large number of configuration parameters that control the Hadoop framework's behavior.

A Hadoop job is often composed of many submodules that implement different algorithms, and some of these sub-modules are connected in serial, while others are connected in parallel. A misconfiguration of the Hadoop framework may impact how all internal tasks coordinate together to achieve tasks. The impact of the settings of all these parameters (which will be covered in *Chapter 2, An Overview of the Hadoop Parameters*) depends on the `map` and `reduce` functions' code, the cluster resources, and of course, the input data.

A MapReduce job performance can also be affected by the number of nodes in the Hadoop cluster and the available resources of all the nodes to run map and reduce tasks. Each node capacity determines the number of mapper and reducer tasks that a node can execute. Therefore, if the resources of nodes are underutilized or overutilized, it will directly impact the MapReduce tasks' performance.

Summary

In this chapter, we learned the MapReduce programing model and reviewed how this works internally. Then, we focused on Hadoop MapReduce and learned about its main components. We also covered internal and external factors that may affect Hadoop MapReduce performance.

In the next chapter, we will investigate Hadoop's tunable parameters and learn about Hadoop metrics and performance tools.

2
An Overview of the Hadoop Parameters

Once you have your Hadoop job running, it is important to know whether your cluster resources are being fully utilized. Fortunately, the Hadoop framework provides several parameters that enable you to tune your job and specify how it will run on the cluster.

Performance tuning involves four main components: CPU utilization, memory occupation, disk I/O, and network traffic. This chapter describes the most relative parameters to these components and introduces techniques to optimize Hadoop execution and define some configuration parameters.

It is important and essential to have an efficient monitoring tool, with alerts delivered when a problem is developing or occurs, which provides a visual indication of how the Hadoop cluster is and has been performing. This chapter is focused on introducing Hadoop performance tuning using configuration parameters and also introducing several tools for monitoring Hadoop services.

In this chapter, we will cover the following topics:

- Investigation of Hadoop tunable parameters
- Hadoop configuration parameters related to CPU utilization, memory, disk I/O, and network
- Hadoop metrics
- Hadoop monitoring tools

Investigating the Hadoop parameters

As discussed in *Chapter 1*, *Understanding MapReduce*, there are many factors that may affect the Hadoop MapReduce performance. In general, workload-dependent Hadoop performance optimization efforts have to focus on three major categories: the system hardware, the system software, and the configuration and tuning/ optimization of the Hadoop infrastructure components.

It is good to point out that Hadoop is classified as a highly-scalable solution, but not necessarily as a high-performance cluster solution. Administrators can configure and tune a Hadoop cluster with various configuration options. Performance configuration parameters focus mainly on CPU utilization, memory occupation, disk I/O, and network traffic. Besides the main performance parameters of Hadoop, other system parameters such as inter-rack bandwidth may affect the overall performance of the cluster.

Hadoop can be configured and customized according to the user's needs; the configuration files that get generated automatically after installation can be modified to meet the specific needs of applications and clusters.

The configuration files fall in two categories: read-only default configuration and site-specific configuration:

- The first category includes `core-default.xml`, `hdfs-default.xml`, and `mapred-default.xml`

- The second category includes `core-site.xml`, `hdfs-site.xml`, and `mapred-site.xml`

There are a large number of variables in Hadoop configuration files that you can define or override in order to control the Hadoop configuration. These variables can be defined in `core-site.xml`, `hdfs-site.xml`, and `mapred-site.xml`. Some variables are used to specify file paths on your system, while others adjust different aspects of the Hadoop framework with different granularity deep inside it. Each configuration file has name-value pairs expressed in an XML format, and they define the workings of different aspects of Hadoop.

From a system's hardware perspective, it is paramount to balance the appropriate hardware components with regard to performance, scalability, and cost. From a software perspective, the choice of the operating system, the **JVM (Java Virtual Machine)**, the specific Hadoop version, as well as other software components that are necessary to run the Hadoop setup do have a profound impact on performance and stability of the environment. The design, setup, configuration, and tuning phases of any Hadoop project are paramount to fully benefit from the distributed Hadoop hardware and software solution stack.

The mapred-site.xml configuration file

The `mapred-site.xml` file may be considered as the main key to enhance the Hadoop MapReduce performance. This configuration file contains CPU, memory, disk I/O, and network-related parameters.

The CPU-related parameters

The following two parameters are the most relative ones to CPU utilization. By overriding these variables, you specify the maximum number of map/reduce tasks that will be run simultaneously by the TaskTracker node. By default, the value of both these parameters is 2.

Configuration variable	Description	Default value
mapred. tasktracker.map. tasks.maximum	It is used to set the maximum number of map tasks that TaskTracker will run simultaneously	2
mapred. tasktracker. reduce.tasks. maximum	It is used to set the maximum number of reduce tasks that TaskTracker will run simultaneously	2

Theoretically, increasing these default values will increase the CPU utilization and therefore improve the performance, but this must be done smartly in accordance with your cluster resources such as CPU (with/without the hyper threading factor) and available memory. Otherwise, you may downgrade the overall MapReduce jobs and the cluster performance.

One typical question asked by users is how many mappers/reducers should be set to achieve best performance? To set this value, you should consider TaskTracker's utilization of resources such as CPU, memory, and disk I/O. Also, you should consider if the job you are running is CPU intensive or not.

To illustrate these parameter settings, assume you have 10 Hadoop cluster nodes and each node has a quad-core CPU. Then, the total number of daemons should be no more than *10 (nodes) x 4 (CPU cores) = 40*. Considering that one CPU core should be reserved for the DataNode daemon and another one for TaskTracker, only 38 CPU cores remain for map/reduce tasks.

You don't need to set the mapper or reducer count to the same value, because it depends on CPU utilization per task and how the job is done by each mapper and reducer to get the final result. You can distribute CPU resources 50 percent for mappers and 50 percent for reducers, use two-third of the CPU resources for mappers and one-third for reducers, or any other distribution scheme that allows you to get your cluster to run optimally.

Setting the count value to -1 means that Hadoop will use all the memory allocated by the administrator for the mapper and reducer tasks. Setting this value larger than the physical CPU cores count will result in intensive CPU context switching (see *Chapter 4, Identifying Resource Weaknesses*), which may considerably downgrade your cluster's performance.

The disk I/O related parameters

In order to optimize disk I/O operations, you may decide to use data compression, which is turned off by default. You can enable compression by changing the default value for parameters that control compression. The `mapred.compress.map.output` variable enables map output compression, the `mapred.output.compress` variable enables job output compression, and the `mapred.map.output.compression.codec` variable is used to define the compression codec.

Configuration variable	Description	Default value
mapred. compress.map. output	This is a Boolean (true or false) value, which is set to `false` by default. If set to `true`, the output of the map tasks will be compressed using the `SequenceFile` codec compression before being sent across the network.	false
mapred.output. compress	This is a Boolean value; setting it to `true` will enable job output compression.	false
mapred.map. output. compression. codec	This value is used to determine the compression codec (coder/decoder) that will be used to compress map outputs.	org.apache. hadoop. io.compress. DefaultCodec

Enabling compressed output for map tasks will reduce the intermediate data volume to write on the storage. Therefore, this will speed up disk write operations in both shuffle and writing phases and reduce the total time of data transfer. Speeding up disk write operations using compression will have an additional CPU cost overhead during the compression/decompression process.

Real-world experience demonstrates that you should enable compression only when your input data is large and easily splittable (such as text files). Otherwise, enabling compression may downgrade the cluster's performance.

To achieve disk I/O balance and greatly improve I/O performance, you can use the feature of writing to multiple locations to write data on all disks on each node. Using multiple physical devices yields roughly 50 percent better performance than RAID 0 striping.

The following two parameters determine where to store data in Hadoop. You may use the `mapred.local.dir` variable to specify where the intermediate map output data is stored, and the `dfs.data.dir` variable to specify where the HDFS data is stored.

Configuration variable	Description	Default value
`mapred.local.dir`	This is used to specify the local directory where we need to store map's intermediate files. You can define multiple directories for this parameter, which should be on separate physical devices. If multiple directories are provided, data is spread over these directories. The directories that do not exist are ignored.	`${hadoop.tmp.dir}/mapred/local`
`dfs.data.dir` (`hdfs-site.xml`)	This is used to specify the directory where the DataNode should store its blocks on the local filesystem. If you provide a comma-delimited list of directories, the data blocks will be stored in all directories. If this parameter is lost, your entire HDFS dataset is lost.	`${hadoop.tmp.dir}/dfs/data`

The memory-related parameters

The memory resource is a very important resource that needs to be allocated smartly in order to avoid swap and allow Hadoop jobs run optimally. You can use memory-related parameters to set the amount of physical memory that you want to reserve to MapReduce jobs. The following table shows the most common memory-related parameters:

Configuration variable	Description	Default value
`mapred.child. java.opts`	This controls the amount of memory available to each JVM task. The default value will reserve 200 MB of memory to run MapReduce jobs.	`-Xmx200m`
`Mapred.child. ulimit`	This parameter is used to control the limit of virtual memory that will be allocated to a MapReduce job.	

The default `Mapred.child.ulimit` value is not specified. If you choose to specify a value for this parameter, then it should be greater than or at least equal to the `-Xmx` value of `mapred.child.java.opts`. Otherwise, the Java Virtual Machine might not start. To set this value correctly, you should set it to a value greater than *2 * mapred. child.java.opts.*

Merging and sorting is another aspect that you can optimize using memory-related parameters. There are three main parameters that you may set to optimize merging and sorting MapReduce performance.

Configuration variable	Description	Default value
`io.sort.mb`	This specifies the amount of buffer space in megabytes to use when sorting streams. When misconfigured, this parameter often causes jobs to run out of memory on small memory machines.	`100`
`io.sort.factor`	This determines the number of map output partitions to merge at a time while sorting files.	`10`
`mapred.job. reduce.input. buffer.percent`	This determines the percentage of memory relative to the maximum heap size to retain map outputs during the reduce phase. The reduce task can begin when the shuffle is concluded, and the allocated memory for any remaining map outputs must be less than this threshold.	`0.0`

If you increase the values of `io.sort.mb` and `io.sort.factor`, it will allocate more memory for sorting and merging operations. This minimizes spills to the disk, which will reduce I/O time for both mapper and reducer tasks. On the other hand, increasing these values increases the memory required by each map task and might increase the garbage collector activities when memory allocated for each task is not large enough.

Our experience shows that you may need to increase the value of `io.sort.factor` if you have large number of spills to the disk, and high I/O times of the sort/shuffle phase. Also, if your map output is large with frequent map-side I/O, you should try to increase the value of `io.sort.mb`. To avoid a "task out of memory" error, you should set `io.sort.mb` to a value greater than *0.25*mapred.child.java.opts* and less than *0.5*mapred.child.java.opts*.

You may increase the value of `mapred.job.reduce.input.buffer.percent` to get more buffer in memory, which will reduce local disk I/O times during the reduce phase, but as stated earlier, if more memory is allocated, it might increase the garbage collector's activities to free unused memory. Therefore, you should try to allocate more memory when map output is large and local disk I/O is frequent during the reduce sort phases.

The network-related parameters

Hadoop has a concept called **rack awareness**. Administrators can define the rack of each DataNode in the cluster. Making Hadoop rack aware is essential because rack awareness prevents data loss and a well rack-aware configuration improves network performance. The variables defined in the following table help make a Hadoop setup rack aware:

Configuration variable	Description	Default value
`mapred.reduce.parallel.copies`	This specifies the number of parallel transfers used to fetch map output during the shuffle phase.	5
`topology.script.file.name (core-site.xml)`	This specifies the script name to be called in order to resolve DNS names to network topology names (for example, pass `host.servers.company` as an argument, and return `/rack1` as the output).	

Increasing `mapred.reduce.parallel.copies` might increase the network flow rate and speed up the process of copying map outputs at the cost of more CPU usage. We suggest increasing this value only if your mapper task produces a very large output.

Hadoop rack awareness is configured using the `topology.script.file.name` parameter in the `core-site.xml` file. This parameter should point to a user-defined script that determines rack-host mapping (Rack1: DataNode1, DataNode2 ... Rack2: DataNode6, DataNode7...). If `topology.script.file.name` is not configured, /`default-rack` is passed for any node's IP address placed on the same rack.

 You may learn more about Hadoop's rack awareness setup and configuration at `http://hadoop.apache.org/docs/r1.2.1/` `cluster_setup.html#Hadoop+Rack+Awareness`

The hdfs-site.xml configuration file

The `hdfs-site.xml` configuration file contains many parameters related to the HDFS storage system that you can override in order to customize your Hadoop installation and/or tune it. The value of the filesystem block size is the most commonly tuned HDFS parameter in `hdfs-site.xml`. It controls the size of the input split, which will be processed by each map task. The size of the input split can be specified through three main variables: `dfs.block.size` (in `hdfs-site.xml`), `mapred.min.split.size`, and `mapred.max.split.size` (both in `mapred-site.xml`).

By default, `dfs.block.size` is set to `67108864` bytes (64 MB). Increasing this value will create larger input splits and therefore reduce the number of blocks that will be stored on each DataNode.

The total number of map tasks depend on the input data size and the total input split size. While map output size is proportional to the HDFS block size, a bigger block size could lead to additional map-side spills if spill-related properties are not adjusted accordingly.

Usually, to maximize throughput, you should adapt the block size to the input data. For a very large input file, it is best to use very large blocks (128 MB or even 256 MB), while for smaller files, using a smaller block size is better. Notice that by changing the `dfs.block.size` parameter, when the file is written, it is possible to have files with different block sizes on the same filesystem (refer to *Chapter 5, Enhancing Map and Reduce Tasks*, to understand the block size impact).

The following table shows the main parameters that you can set in the `hdfs-site.` `xml` configuration file:

Configuration variable	Description	Default value
dfs.access. time.precision	This is the precision, in milliseconds, of the access times that are maintained. If this value is 0, no access times are maintained. The default value is 1 hour. To disable access time for HDFS, set this to 0 (zero), which may increase performance on busy clusters where bottlenecks often occur due to slow log writing speeds on NameNode.	3600000
dfs.balance. bandwidthPerSec	This specifies the maximum amount of bandwidth that each DataNode may utilize to rebalance block storage among Hadoop cluster's DataNodes. This value is expressed in bytes per second.	1048576
dfs.block.size	This is the default block size for new files. This parameter should be tuned depending on your cluster and your data jobs.	67108864
dfs.data.dir	This determines the location on the local filesystem where a data node should store its blocks. If a comma-delimited list of directories can be provided, then data will be stored in all named directories. If this data is lost, your entire HDFS data set is lost.	${hadoop. tmp.dir}/ dfs/data
dfs.datanode. du.reserved	This is the amount of space that must be kept free in each location used for block storage.	0.0
dfs.datanode. handler.count	This determines the number of server threads handling block requests. If you increase this value, this may increase the DataNode throughput, in particular if it stores its blocks on multiple separate physical devices.	3
dfs.max.objects	This variable determines the maximum number of objects (files, directories, and blocks) permitted. By default, this variable is set to zero, which indicates no limit to the number of objects.	0
dfs.name.dir	This variable supports individual directory path or a comma-separated list of directories to use for data block storage. Hadoop will process this list using a round-robin algorithm for storing new data blocks. To get better performance, these locations should be set to point to separate physical devices.	${hadoop. tmp.dir}/ dfs/name

Configuration variable	Description	Default value
dfs.name.edits.dir	This determines where on the NameNode the transaction (edits) file should be stored. Ideally, for redundancy, you can define a comma-delimited list of directories to replicate the transaction file in all the directories. The default value is the same as dfs.name.dir.	${dfs.name.dir}
dfs.namenode.handler.count	This specifies the number of server threads for the NameNode. You should increase this value if you have a large and busy cluster.	10
dfs.replication	This determines the default block replication number of each block stored on the cluster. This number can be specified when the file is created. Defining a large value allows more DataNodes to fail before blocks are unavailable; however, this will increase the amount of network I/O required to store data and the disk space requirements. This may also increase the probability that a map task will have a local replica of the input split.	3
dfs.replication.considerLoad	This is a Boolean value that is used to decide the DataNode load when picking replication locations.	true

Changing the block size will impact a number of things. In most cases, splitting a file with large block size will produce fewer blocks. Therefore, this will reduce the metadata of the NameNode, which is important with very large files. Moreover, it will be possible for a client to read/write more data without interacting with the NameNode.

With fewer blocks, you need fewer nodes to store the file. This may reduce total throughput for parallel access and make the scheduling of data-local tasks more difficult.

Reducing the parallel throughput also means you may not gain maximum parallelism, which can decrease overhead and your cluster may be underutilized. This increases the chance of straggling of tasks, and if a task fails, more work needs to be redone.

Also, having fewer blocks means having more data to process per task, which can cause additional read/write operations.

The core-site.xml configuration file

The `core-site.xml` file is one of the major Hadoop configuration files and contains the configurations common to the whole Hadoop distribution. It exists on every host in your cluster.

Basically, the variables of `core-site.xml` allow you to override or define the distributed filesystem name, the temporary directory, and some other parameters related to the network configuration.

Configuration variables	Description	Default value
`fs.default.name`	This determines the name (URI) of the default filesystem. This should be `hdfs://NameNodeHostName:PORT`.	`file:///`
`hadoop.tmp.dir`	This determines the path to store temporary files.	`/tmp/hadoop-${user.name}`
`fs.checkpoint.dir`	It determines a list of directories where the secondary NameNode stores checkpoints. It stores a copy of the checkpoint in each directory in the list.	`${hadoop.tmp.dir}/dfs/namesecondary`
`io.file.buffer.size`	This determines the amount of buffered data during read/write operations on the disk files. The size of this buffer is typically a multiple of the hardware page size (4096 on Intel x86).	`4096`

In the case of small clusters, all servers are usually connected by a single switch. Therefore, there are only two locality levels: **on-machine** and **off-machine**. When loading data from HDFS into the DataNode's local drive, the NameNode will schedule only one copy to be transferred into the local DataNode, and will randomly pick two other machines from the cluster for storing a replica of the data.

For larger Hadoop clusters that span multiple racks, it is important to ensure that replicas of data exist on all racks. Then, a switch failure will not render the data blocks unavailable due to replicas being available.

The `io.file.buffer.size` parameter sets the buffer size used by Hadoop during I/O operations. This parameter is set by default to `4096` bytes (4 KB). On modern systems, it can be increased to `65536` bytes (64 KB) or `131072` bytes (128 KB) for performance gains.

Hadoop MapReduce metrics

Due to its scale and distributed nature, diagnosing the performance problems of Hadoop programs and monitoring a Hadoop system are inherently difficult. Although Hadoop system exports many textual metrics and logs, this information may be difficult to interpret and not fully understood by many application programmers.

Currently, Hadoop reports coarse-grained metrics about the performance of the whole system through logs and metrics API. Unfortunately, it lacks important metrics for per-job/per-task levels such as disk and network I/O utilization. In the case of running multiple jobs in a Hadoop system, it also lacks metrics to reflect the cluster resource utilization of each task. This results in difficulty for cluster administrators to measure their cluster utilization and set up the correct configuration of Hadoop systems.

Furthermore, logs generated by Hadoop can get excessively large, which makes it extremely difficult to handle them manually and can hardly answer the simple question: "why can a specific number of mappers/reducers not achieve optimal throughput?" The following screenshot shows a partial Hadoop job history view in some detail:

	Counter	Map	Reduce	Total
	Launched reduce tasks	0	0	3
	SLOTS_MILLIS_MAPS	0	0	814,793
	Total time spent by all reduces waiting after reserving slots (ms)	0	0	0
Job Counters	Total time spent by all maps waiting after reserving slots (ms)	0	0	0
	Launched map tasks	0	0	16
	Data-local map tasks	0	0	16
	SLOTS_MILLIS_REDUCES	0	0	983,705
File Input Format Counters	Bytes Read	1,048,633,344	0	1,048,633,344
File Output Format Counters	Bytes Written	0	1,048,576,000	1,048,576,000
	FILE_BYTES_READ	1,069,697,018	1,069,547,574	2,139,244,592
	HDFS_BYTES_READ	1,048,634,848	0	1,048,634,848
FileSystemCounters	FILE_BYTES_WRITTEN	2,140,021,926	1,069,720,710	3,209,742,636

Performance monitoring tools

Monitoring basic system resources on Hadoop cluster nodes such as CPU utilization and average disk data transfer rates helps to understand the overall utilization of these hardware resources and identify any bottlenecks while diagnosing performance issues. Monitoring a Hadoop cluster includes monitoring the usage of system resources on cluster nodes along with monitoring the key service metrics. The most commonly monitored resources are I/O bandwidth, number of disk I/O operations per second, average data transfer rate, network latency, and average memory and swap space utilization.

Hadoop performance monitoring suggests collecting performance counters' data in order to determine whether the response times of various tasks lie within acceptable execution time range. The average percentage utilization for MapReduce tasks and HDFS storage capacity over time indicates whether your cluster's resources are used optimally or are underused.

Hadoop offers a substantial number of metrics and information sources for monitoring and debugging of Hadoop services. It requires correlating and collecting these system and service metrics from the cluster nodes to analyze the overall state of the Hadoop cluster along with diagnosing any problems that are discovered.

You may enhance your monitoring experience by using proven open source monitoring systems such as **Chukwa**, **Ganglia**, **Nagios**, and **Ambari** (a nonexhaustive list) to consolidate various metrics and information sources provided by Hadoop into more meaningful service-specific summary, graphs, and alerts.

Using Chukwa to monitor Hadoop

Chukwa (`http://incubator.apache.org/chukwa/`) is an open source data collection system for monitoring and analyzing large distributed systems. It is built on top of Hadoop and includes a powerful and flexible toolkit for monitoring, analyzing, and viewing results.

Many components of Chukwa are pluggable, allowing easy customization and enhancement. It provides a standardized framework for processing the collected data and can scale to thousands of nodes in both collection and analysis capacities.

Using Ganglia to monitor Hadoop

Ganglia (`http://ganglia.sourceforge.net/`) was originally developed at the University of California, Berkeley. Its purpose is to provide a robust and resource-consuming solution to monitor a computing cluster's performance. This cluster can contain hundreds or thousands of nodes. Basically, Ganglia collects high-level variables such as CPU utilization and free disk space for each monitored node. Also, it can be used to monitor failed cluster nodes.

The current Hadoop version has built-in support for Ganglia (version 3.0+). It is a highly scalable cluster monitoring tool that provides graphical view information about the state of a single cluster or set of clusters, or individual machines in a cluster.

Ganglia's architecture and implementation on Hadoop supports federations of clusters, monitoring the state within each cluster and aggregating those states. The architecture includes a **Ganglia Collector** that runs monitoring daemons and collects metrics for each cluster. It also runs a meta daemon that aggregates the metrics for all clusters. The Ganglia Collector provides a web user interface that presents real-time dynamic views of memory usage, disk usage, network statistics, running processes, and other metrics.

Using Nagios to monitor Hadoop

Nagios (http://www.nagios.org/) is a popular open source monitoring tool system, which is heavily used in **High Performance Computing** (**HPC**) and other environments, and is designed to obtain system resources metrics. You can use it to monitor your Hadoop cluster resources and the status of applications and operating system attributes, such as CPU usage, disk space, and memory utilization.

Nagios has an integrated built-in notification system that focuses on alerting rather than gathering and tracking system metrics (such as Ganglia). The current version of Nagios allows you to run agents on target hosts and provides a flexible and customizable framework for collecting metrics and information data about the state of your Hadoop cluster.

Nagios can be used to address different monitoring perspectives:

- Getting instant information about your Hadoop infrastructure organization
- Raising and receiving alerts on system failures
- Analyzing, reporting, and producing graphs on cluster utilization and making decisions about future hardware acquisitions
- Detecting and anticipating future issues
- Monitoring how exhausted the queues are and finding the availability of nodes for running the jobs

 Nagios is to be considered as a health checking and alerting monitoring tool.

Using Apache Ambari to monitor Hadoop

The Apache Ambari project (`http://incubator.apache.org/ambari/`) simplifies Hadoop management and cluster monitoring. Its primary goal is to simplify the deployment and management of Hadoop clusters in multi-instance environments.

Ambari provides a set of intuitive and easy-to-use tools to monitor Hadoop clusters, hiding the complexities of the Hadoop framework. It exposes RESTful APIs for administrators to allow integration with other system(s). Furthermore, Ambari relies on measures from Ganglia and Nagios for an alert system function to send e-mails to the attention of the administrator when required (for example, when a node fails, the remaining disk space is low, and so on). Additionally, Ambari supports Hadoop security by supporting installation of secure (Kerberos-based) Hadoop clusters, providing role-based user authentication, authorization, auditing, and integration with LDAP and Active Directory for user management.

> If you set up your Hadoop cluster through Apache Ambari, you can also use it to set up monitoring tools such as Ganglia or Nagios.

Summary

In this chapter, we discussed Hadoop MapReduce performance tuning and learned how application developers and cluster administrators can tune Hadoop in order to enhance the MapReduce job's performance.

We learned about most configuration variables related to CPU, disk I/O, memory and network utilization and discussed how these variables may affect the MapReduce job's performance.

Then, we learned about Hadoop metrics and suggested some open source monitoring tools, which enhance the Hadoop monitoring experience and are very handy to Hadoop cluster administrators and application developers.

In the next chapter, we will learn how to identify resource bottlenecks based on performance indicators and also learn about common performance tuning methods.

3
Detecting System Bottlenecks

How do you know whether your Hadoop MapReduce job is performing its work optimally? One of the most common performance-related requests we receive in our consulting practice is to find out why a specific job took a long time to execute, and to troubleshoot bottleneck incidents.

In *Chapter 1, Understanding Hadoop MapReduce*, and *Chapter 2, An Overview of the Hadoop Parameters*, we learned about factors that may impact Hadoop MapReduce performance and Hadoop MapReduce common parameters' settings. In this chapter, we will continue our journey and learn how to detect potential system bottlenecks.

This chapter presents the performance tuning process, the importance of creating a baseline before any tuning job, and how to use this baseline to tune your cluster. You will also learn how to identify resource bottlenecks and what to do in order to break these bottlenecks.

In this chapter, we will cover the following:

- Introducing the performance tuning process
- Creating a performance baseline
- Hadoop cluster tuning approach
- Identifying system-resource bottlenecks

Performance tuning

The fundamental goal of performance tuning is to ensure that all available resources (CPU, RAM, I/O, and network) in a given cluster configuration are available to a particular job and are used in a balanced way.

Hadoop MapReduce resources are classified into categories such as computation, memory, network bandwidth, and input/output storage. If any of these resources perform badly, this will impact Hadoop's performance, which may cause your jobs to run slowly. Therefore, tuning Hadoop MapReduce performance is getting balanced resources on your Hadoop cluster and not just tuning one or more variables.

In simple words, tuning a Hadoop MapReduce job process consists of multiple analyses that investigate the Hadoop metrics and indicators in order to learn about execution time, memory amount used, and the number of bytes to read or store in the local filesystem, and so on.

Hadoop performance tuning is an iterative process. You launch a job, then analyzes Hadoop counters, adjust them, and re-run the job. Then repeat this process until you reach the ultimate performance of your Hadoop cluster. The following steps describe this process:

1. Create a baseline, as you first need to evaluate the overall system performance. You will run your job the first time using the default configuration settings of your Hadoop cluster. This will be your baseline.

   After you have this baseline, you will begin tuning the variable values to execute jobs optimally. So, we can say that performance tuning is the primary means of measuring and analyzing where time is consumed.

2. You analyze the Hadoop counters, modify and tune some configuration settings, and then re-run the job. The result is compared to the baseline. When the analysis is complete, you can review the results and accept or reject the inferences.

3. Repeat step 2 until you get the shortest execution time for your job.

The following figure illustrates the Hadoop performance tuning process:

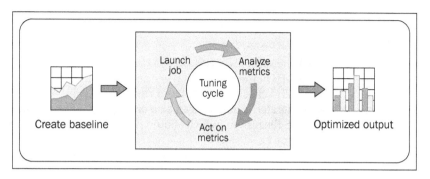

Creating a performance baseline

Let's begin by creating a performance baseline for our system. When creating a baseline, you should keep the Hadoop default configuration settings and use the TeraSort benchmark tool, which is a part of the example JAR files provided with the Hadoop distribution package. TeraSort is accepted as an industry standard benchmark to compare the performance of Hadoop. This benchmark tool tries to use the entire Hadoop cluster to sort 1 TB of data as quickly as possible and is divided into three main modules:

- **TeraGen**: This module is used to generate a file of the desired size as an input that usually ranges between 500 GB up to 3 TB. Once the input data is generated by TeraGen, it can be used in all the runs with the same file size.

- **TeraSort**: This module will sort the input file across the Hadoop cluster. TeraSort stresses the Hadoop cluster on both layers, MapReduce and HDFS, in terms of computation, network bandwidth, and I/O response. Once sorted, a single reduced task is created to check the output of the sort phase for validity.

- **TeraValidate**: This module is used for accuracy and to verify the sorted data.

In order to run the TeraSort benchmark tool and get a baseline, you first need to generate the sample input data that will be sorted by TeraSort. Run TeraGen to generate a file with 10 GB size (depending on your cluster capacity, you may generate a larger file size up to 3 TB) using the following command line where you specify the file size ($104857600 = 10$ GB) and the output DFS directory (/data/input):

```
hadoop jar $HADOOP_PREFIX/hadoop-*examples*.jar teragen 104857600 /data/
input
```

The /data/input HDFS directory must be empty, otherwise you will get a Java Exception error. If not already empty, you can clear this directory using the following command line:

```
hadoop dfs -rmr /data/input
```

To check whether the sample data files have been generated correctly, open the Hadoop DFS home page (http://machinename:50070/dfshealth.jsp) and check the **DFS Used** row, which should reflect the size of your generated data. You can also browse the /data/input directory in the DFS filesystem, which should contain all the generated files (part-0000 - part-00*).

Once the input data is generated, run TeraSort using the following command line, which specifies the input and output data folders:

```
hadoop jar $HADOOP_PREFIX/hadoop-*examples*.jar terasort /data/input /
data/output
```

The only true way to optimize and tune your cluster is to analyze the counters, change the settings' configuration, re-run your MapReduce job, and then come back to change the settings and re-run the job until you lower the finishing time to the lowest possible value.

When the TeraSort job completes, you get a performance baseline. We can now move to the iterative step (discussed in the previous section) and then analyze these settings.

To illustrate how to use this performance baseline, let's assume we want to process a 10 GB file on a three-node Hadoop cluster (each node has one CPU with four cores, 4 GB RAM, and 40 GB HDD space). Based on the default settings (reported in the following table) this job took 4 minutes and 3 seconds.

This is a light Hadoop cluster with medium data size context. Therefore, the cluster can be configured as follows:

- The replication factor can be reduced to 2.
- The block size can be increased up to 128 MB.
- The io.sort.factor parameter depends on the available memory on the node. Each node has 4 GB of memory; therefore, we can allow more memory to the intermediate map data.
- The io.sort.mb value should be *io.sort.factor* * 10 that is 35 * 10 = 350 MB, which is the size that will be allowed to map intermediate data.

- The value of `mapred.tasktracker.map.tasks.maximum` and `mapred.tasktracker.reduce.tasks.maximum` can be set to the CPU core number minus one. Thus, the value should be *4 - 1 = 3*.

- It is advisable to set the value of `mapred.reduce.tasks` between 50 percent and 99 percent of the cluster capacity so that all reduce tasks finish in one wave. This parameter may therefore be set to *0.95 * 3 (nodes) * 3 = 8.55* reducer slots, which is rounded down to 8.

The default value of `mapred.child.java.opts` can be increased to 500 MB to allow more memory to mapper and reducer tasks. However, this should not exceed the available RAM on the node. Therefore, you can set this value using the formula: *(mapred.tasktracker.map.tasks.maximum + mapred.tasktracker.reduce.tasks.maximum) * memory to allocate (in MB) < available RAM - reserved memory, that is, (3 + 3) * 500 < 4096 - 350 (reserved intermediate map output)*.

Now we re-run the same MapReduce job again, report the configured settings, and compare the results to those of the baseline. We can choose to accept the tuning results or reject them and re-tune the settings again until we are satisfied with the results.

All these setting values are summarized in the following table:

Hadoop parameter	Baseline	Tuned1	Tuned2	Tuned3
`dfs.replication`	3	2		
`dfs.block.size`	67108864	134217728		
`dfs.namenode.handler.count`	10	20		
`dfs.datanode.handler.count`	3	5		
`io.sort.factor`	10	35		
`io.sort.mb`	100	350		
`mapred.tasktracker.map.tasks.maximum`	2	3		
`mapred.map.tasks`	2	2		
`mapred.reduce.tasks`	1	8		
`mapred.tasktracker.reduce.tasks.maximum`	2	3		
`mapred.reduce.parallel.copies`	5	5		
`mapred.job.reduce.input.buffer.percent`	0	0		
`mapred.child.java.opts`	-Xmx200m	-Xmx500m		

Hadoop parameter	Baseline	Tuned1	Tuned2	Tuned3
...				
Input data size	10 GB	10 GB		
Cluster's node number	3	3		
Job execution time (sec)	243	185		
Improvement over baseline (percent)		23.86%		

Identifying resource bottlenecks

Typically, a bottleneck occurs when one resource of the system consumes more time than required to finish its tasks and forces other resources to wait, which decreases the overall system performance.

Prior to any deep-dive action into tuning your Hadoop cluster, it is a good practice to ensure that your cluster is stable and your MapReduce jobs are operational. We suggest you verify that the hardware components of your cluster are configured correctly and if necessary, upgrade any software components of the Hadoop stack to the latest stable version. You may also perform a MapReduce job such as TeraSort or PI Estimator to stress your cluster. This is a very important step to get a healthy and optimized Hadoop cluster.

Once your cluster hardware and software components are well configured and updated, you need to create a baseline performance stress-test. In order to stress your Hadoop cluster, you can use the Hadoop microbenchmarks such as TeraSort, TestDFSIO, NNBench, or MRBench. All these benchmarks are part of the Hadoop distribution package.

However, remember that a MapReduce job is in fact a pipeline with many stages, and each stage requires different types of resources. The following illustration describes the major resources (CPU, RAM, I/O, and network bandwidth) that are required by Hadoop to complete a MapReduce job and may create a potential resource bottleneck.

		RAM	CPU	Storage I/O	Network
Map phase	Input	✔		✔	
	Computation	✔	✔		
	Partition and sort	✔		✔	
	Output	✔		✔	
Reduce phase	Copying Map output	✔		✔	✔
	Computation	✔	✔		
	Output	✔		✔	✔

Identifying RAM bottlenecks

The RAM (memory) is a potential bottleneck source that may have significant effects on your MapReduce job performance. The amount of memory available on each node should be enough to handle the needs of the job to process. You need to ensure that the memory of the cluster nodes is properly configured and set. Otherwise, in an intensive workload context, the Map and Reduce tasks might be initiated but immediately fail. Also, when Hadoop does not have enough memory to handle data, it will use the system storage to store its data and these swaps between memory and storage may be time consuming and will slow down the system.

In order to identify a potential memory bottleneck, you should highlight, using a monitoring tool (such as Ganglia, vmstat), the usage of the swap memory. This will help you to identify whether your map and reduce tasks have enough memory to accomplish their job or not. Otherwise, you should probably extend the node's physical memory or adjust the number of mappers and reducers.

The following screenshot shows the vmstat output report, which shows the amount of memory swapped to disk (so column) and the amount of memory swapped from disk (si column):

```
khaled@HNName:/usr/local/hadoop/bin$ vmstat -S M 1
procs ----------memory---------- --swap-- ----io---- -system-- ----cpu----
 r  b   swpd   free   buff  cache   si   so    bi    bo   in   cs us sy id wa
 0  0    378    637     32    191    0    0     0     0  313  586  1  1 99  0
 1  0    378    637     32    191    0    0     0     0  398  761  2  1 97  0
 1  0    378    637     32    191    0    0     0     0  320  646  2  2 96  0
```

In *Chapter 4, Identifying Resource Weaknesses*, you will learn how to configure the number of map and reduce tasks depending on the physical memory you have on each node.

Identifying CPU bottlenecks

CPU is the key resource when processing data in both Map and Reduce computation stages. An intensive CPU activity may be the result of an intensive computation in map and/or reduce user function's code. This high CPU utilization may be a potential bottleneck. Also, a CPU may often be idle if it needs to wait for other resources to feed data before it can be processed. This is generally caused by a misconfiguration of the map and reduce tasks and the Hadoop framework underutilizing the CPU resource. The symptoms of a CPU bottleneck aren't difficult to recognize. Usually, a processor load (time) often exceeds 90 percent; and on multiprocessor systems, the total processor load (time) exceeds 50 percent. But, these symptoms don't always indicate a processor problem.

To identify whether your node deals with very high CPU activity, you should examine all processes and threads actually run by the processor using your monitoring tool. Then you should identify whether there is a particular process that monopolizes the CPU and understand why it does so. Tuning map and reduce tasks' numbers may resolve the bottleneck, and as a last resort you may need to upgrade to a faster processor or add additional processors, which is a benefit for the overall MapReduce job.

Identifying storage bottlenecks

Storage I/O is the second most common bottleneck source and unfortunately, this resource is needed by the Hadoop in many stages of the MapReduce pipeline process. Storage resource can decrease MapReduce job performance and become a bottleneck at every stage of the execution pipeline. Prior to any storage tuning action, it is recommended to benchmark your storage to learn about its I/O throughput capabilities. You can do this by running the Hadoop HDFS benchmark TestDFSIO which is a read/write test for HDFS. Also, to run a distributed benchmark, you can use DFSCIOTest, which is an I/O distributed benchmark of libhdfs.

Storage bottlenecks appear as sustained rates of disk activity above 85 percent. But this symptom may also be the result of a memory or CPU bottleneck, which looks like a disk bottleneck. This is why you should first check if there is any memory or a CPU bottleneck before trying to identify a disk bottleneck.

Using the TestDFSIO benchmark tool will help you to know how fast your cluster's NameNode and DataNode storage are. The following figure shows a typical TestDFSIO output log:

```
fs.TestDFSIO: ----- TestDFSIO ----- : write
fs.TestDFSIO:            Date & time: Sat Jan 04 06:00:22 CET 2014
fs.TestDFSIO:         Number of files: 10
fs.TestDFSIO: Total MBytes processed: 1000
fs.TestDFSIO:      Throughput mb/sec: 13.439595736960232
fs.TestDFSIO: Average IO rate mb/sec: 16.07526206970215
fs.TestDFSIO:  IO rate std deviation: 10.489540906701501
fs.TestDFSIO:     Test exec time sec: 95.83

fs.TestDFSIO: ----- TestDFSIO ----- : read
fs.TestDFSIO:            Date & time: Sat Jan 04 06:22:32 CET 2014
fs.TestDFSIO:         Number of files: 10
fs.TestDFSIO: Total MBytes processed: 1000
fs.TestDFSIO:      Throughput mb/sec: 25.343403112169902
fs.TestDFSIO: Average IO rate mb/sec: 33.82097625732422
fs.TestDFSIO:  IO rate std deviation: 27.928920882163286
fs.TestDFSIO:     Test exec time sec: 86.047
```

To launch a read/write benchmark test using TestDFSIO, you can use the following command line, which writes/reads 10 files of 1000 MB each.

```
hadoop jar hadoop-test.jar TestDFSIO -write -nrFiles 10
  -fileSize 1000
```

```
hadoop jar hadoop-test.jar TestDFSIO -read -nrFiles 10 -fileSize 1000
```

Therefore, using log information output of TestDFSIO, you can calculate the storage throughput using the following formula:

*Total read throughput and total write throughput = number of files * throughput (mb/sec).*

In *Chapter 4, Identifying Resource Weaknesses,* you will learn how to determine the storage capacity for a given node.

Identifying network bandwidth bottlenecks

The network bandwidth may also be a possible bottleneck source. Usually, this bottleneck occurs when you have to transfer a large amount of data over the network. In the Hadoop context, this bottleneck occurs when a large amount of data is present. High network utilization happens when reduce tasks pull data from map tasks in the shuffle phase, and also when the job outputs the final results into HDFS.

For the storage system, it is recommended to stress your Hadoop cluster in order to learn about your network bandwidth capabilities and ensure that the network utilization will not become a bottleneck when used in a particular job. The network bandwidth needs to be constantly monitored to be able to figure out whether your data can be transferred efficiently between your cluster's nodes.

To analyze your system's performance, you can also use the Linux OS utilities such as `dstat`, `top`, `htop`, `iotop`, `vmstat`, `iostat`, `sar`, or `netstat`, which are helpful in capturing system-level performance statistics. Then you use the collected data to study how different resources of the cluster are being utilized by the Hadoop jobs, and which resources create a bottleneck or may be under contention.

To identify and conduct a deep-dive analysis on potential performance bottlenecks induced by software and/or hardware events, you can also use Linux profilers such as `perf` or `strace`.

The network performance analysis is a follow-up to other monitoring efforts. In general, you should start by checking your networking hardware including external elements such as cables, hubs, switches, among others. Then, ensure that you are using the most current network adapters and latest device driver's version for your network components. You should also check the configuration of your network and ensure that it is set to the highest and widest bandwidth possible.

To identify potential network bandwidth bottlenecks, you should monitor and check your network data and interrupt rates (the amount of sent and received bytes over your network interface card). If the data rate is close to or equal to one-eighth of the available bandwidth, it can be inferred that this may be the sign of an overloaded network. Also, a high rate of interrupts means your system is being overloaded by interrupts due to network traffic.

 You can check your network traffic data and interrupt rates using dstat as dstat --nf to display data rates, and dstat -i or dstat -if to display interrupt rates.

Summary

In this chapter, we introduced the performance tuning process cycle and learned about Hadoop counters. We covered the TeraSort benchmark with its TeraGen module and learned to generate a performance baseline that will be used as a reference when tuning the Hadoop cluster. We also learned the approach to tune a Hadoop cluster illustrated by a three-node Hadoop cluster example and suggested tuning some setting parameters to improve the cluster's performance.

Then we moved ahead and discussed resource bottlenecks and what component is involved at each MapReduce stage or may potentially be the source of a bottleneck. For each component (CPU, RAM, storage, and network bandwidth), we learned how to identify system bottlenecks with suggestions to try to eliminate them.

In the next chapter, we will learn how to identify Hadoop cluster resource weaknesses and how to configure a Hadoop cluster correctly. Keep reading!

4
Identifying Resource Weaknesses

Every Hadoop cluster consists of different machines and different hardware. This means that each Hadoop installation should be optimized for its unique cluster setup. To ensure that your Hadoop is performing jobs efficiently, you need to check your cluster and identify potential bottlenecks in order to eliminate them.

This chapter presents some scenarios and techniques to identify cluster weaknesses. We will then introduce some formulas that will help to determine an optimal configuration for NameNodes and DataNodes. After that, you will learn how to configure your cluster correctly and how to determine the number of mappers and reducers for your cluster.

In this chapter, you will learn the following:

- To check the cluster's weakness based on some scenarios
- To identify CPU contention and inappropriate number of mappers and reducers
- To identify massive I/O and network traffic
- To size your cluster and define its sizing
- To configure your cluster correctly

Identifying cluster weakness

Adapting the Hadoop framework's configuration based on a cluster's hardware and number of nodes has proven to give increased performance. In order to ensure that your Hadoop framework is using your hardware efficiently and you have defined the number of mappers and reducers correctly, you need to check your environment to identify whether there are nodes, CPU, or network weaknesses. Then you can decide whether the Hadoop framework should behave as a new set of configuration, or needs to be optimized.

In the following sections, we will go through common scenarios that may cause your job to perform poorly. Each scenario has its own technique that shows how to identify the problem. The scenario covers the cluster node's health, the input data size, massive I/O and network traffic, insufficient concurrent tasks, and CPU contention (which occurs when all lower priority tasks have to wait when any higher priority CPU-bound task is running, and there are no other CPUs that can handle other work).

Checking the Hadoop cluster node's health

Often in multi-node Hadoop clusters, it is possible that a node may fail due to a hardware failure such as hard disk failure or a power supply failure. In this case, the node cannot be used by Hadoop to process jobs and the node will be marked as **Blacklisted**, **Graylisted**, or **Excluded** by the framework. This can also happen in a single node cluster. In such a case, the node is down and you cannot process any MapReduce jobs. Checking whether Hadoop is using all the nodes of your cluster is the first step to get full performance from your cluster.

To determine whether you have unused nodes in your cluster, you should check the cluster summary displayed on your JobTracker page. The cluster summary must show **0** nodes for each of the **Blacklisted Nodes**, **Graylisted Nodes**, and **Excluded Nodes**. The following screenshot shows a partial cluster summary in which appears the Blacklisted, Graylisted, and Excluded nodes:

Blacklisted Nodes	Graylisted Nodes	Excluded Nodes
0	0	0

Your cluster should not have any unused nodes.

The excluded nodes are ignored by the Hadoop framework and are not permitted to connect to the cluster. Also, Hadoop doesn't schedule any jobs to process to the Blacklisted nodes and they don't contribute to the cluster; removing the Blacklisted nodes from the cluster can have a significant impact on the job's performance.

The Graylisted nodes are nodes that have intermittent failures (which may become permanent) and will affect your job's performance and execution time due to failing tasks. You should quickly react to the node failures by replacing or removing them. While Excluded nodes are controlled by the administrator by maintaining the `dfs.hosts.exclude` property (for HDFS) and the `mapred.hosts.exclude` property (for MapReduce), it's a good practice to set up monitoring for Blacklisted and Graylisted nodes using Hadoop cluster management tools such **Nagios**, **Ganglia**, or **Cacti**.

Checking the input data size

In some cases, you may run your MapReduce job that takes a certain amount of time to process data, and if you rerun the same job, you will observe that it takes longer to process the input data. This is not necessarily due to the inefficient implementation of a map function or a resource bottleneck, but may be due to the input data that has grown between the first and the second run. This may occur, for example, if you're running a web log processing job on a particular day and this day the logfile is much larger than normal logfiles, which may be the reason for slowness of your map job.

To identify whether there are different volumes of input data sizes in your map (or reduce) input sizes, you can compare the map input and output data sizes of the slow job with the input and output sizes of the baseline of your previous jobs. Basically, you need to compare four counters: **HDFS_BYTES_WRITTEN**, **Reduce shuffle bytes**, **Map output bytes**, and **Map input bytes**.

The following screenshot shows the Hadoop counters you need to focus on and compare their values with those of your baseline values:

Counter	Map	Reduce	Total
FILE_BYTES_READ	1,069,697,118	1,069,547,174	2,139,244,592
HDFS_BYTES_READ	1,069,634,848	0	1,069,634,848
FILE_BYTES_WRITTEN	2,169,021,962	1,069,735,713	3,209,742,655
HDFS_BYTES_WRITTEN	0	1,069,574,000	1,069,574,000
Map output materialized bytes	0	0	1,069,547,000
Map input records	0	0	16,605,760
Reduce shuffle bytes	0	0	1,069,547,000
Spilled Records	0	0	33,417,290
Map output bytes	0	0	1,069,574,000
Total committed heap usage (bytes)	0	0	1,854,235,392
CPU time spent (ms)	0	0	467,620
Map input bytes	0	0	1,069,574,000
SPLIT_RAW_BYTES	1,504	0	1,504

Checking massive I/O and network traffic

As discussed in *Chapter 3, Detecting System Bottlenecks*, bottlenecks on disk I/O or network bandwidth could cause a slow job performance or even Java exceptions (often time-out exception). Massive I/O can occur either while reading the input data or while writing the output data. If the disk I/O or network traffic does not have a high throughput, computation resources are constrained to wait for the incoming data and will spend time waiting to get data to process.

Bottlenecks may occur while reading very large input data which may constrain mappers to wait (or to be idle) before they can process the input data. To identify massive I/O due to large input data, you should focus on two Hadoop counter values: **FILE_BYTES_READ** and **HDFS_BYTES_READ**. These counter values should be huge if you have a very large input data.

The following screenshot shows the Hadoop counters you should focus on in order to identify a massive I/O due to large input data:

	Counter	Map	Reduce	Total
File Output Format Counters	Bytes Written	0	0	1,048,576,000
FileSystemCounters	FILE_BYTES_READ	1,069,697,018	1,069,547,574	2,139,244,592
	HDFS_BYTES_READ	1,048,634,848	0	1,048,634,848
	FILE_BYTES_WRITTEN	2,140,021,974	1,069,720,719	3,209,742,693
	HDFS_BYTES_WRITTEN	0	1,048,576,000	1,048,576,000

Massive I/O can also be caused by a large output data. This usually occurs when reducers write their output to HDFS, which requires a lot of I/O write operations. To identify any massive bottleneck I/O or network traffic, you can check the **Bytes Written** and **HDFS_BYTES_WRITTEN** Hadoop counter values if you see huge numbers. If such bottlenecks occur, you should observe high values for both counters. The following screenshot shows the counters that you should give a particular attention to identify massive I/O and network traffic caused by large output data:

	Counter	Map	Reduce	Total
File Output Format Counters	Bytes Written	0	0	1,048,576,000
FileSystemCounters	FILE_BYTES_READ	1,069,697,018	1,069,547,574	2,139,244,592
	HDFS_BYTES_READ	1,048,634,848	0	1,048,634,848
	FILE_BYTES_WRITTEN	2,140,021,974	1,069,720,719	3,209,742,693
	HDFS_BYTES_WRITTEN	0	1,048,576,000	1,048,576,000

You should also consider the replication factor (which is configured through the `dfs.replication` parameter). It determines the default block replication number of each block stored in the cluster (see *Chapter 2, An Overview of the Hadoop Parameters*). If your replication factor is greater than one, it means more data to read/write and the data will be replicated across the network. Therefore, you will usually observe high values in counters for both I/O and network usage.

To resolve any massive I/O or network bandwidth bottleneck, you can compress data or use combiners. These techniques will be discussed in *Chapter 6, Optimizing MapReduce Tasks*.

Checking for insufficient concurrent tasks

Poor MapReduce job configuration may leave many resources idle. Basically, concurrent tasks are determined by the total capacity of Map and Reduce slots for the cluster, and the number of Map and Reduce jobs defined to process a particular job.

If there is a misconfiguration for the concurrent tasks either for the cluster or the job, the CPU resource will often be idle or overloaded to this misconfiguration. The most commonly observed misconfiguration is leaving the CPU's cores in a cluster idle with no work assigned to them. This misconfiguration may also lead to underutilized I/O throughput and network bandwidth, because there are no requests coming from the CPU cores. If you have misconfigured your cluster or job capacity, you will observe a low CPU utilization on your DataNodes.

To check underutilization configuration, you should focus on the Hadoop **Num Tasks**, **Running**, **Map Task Capacity**, and **Reduce Task Capacity** counters, which are helpful to check whether you are using your CPU's cores to their full capacity or not. The **Map Task Capacity** and **Reduce Task Capacity** values should be set at least to the CPU's cores number, that is 1.

The following screenshot shows a partial cluster summary (**Map Task Capacity** and **Reduce Task Capacity**) from the MapReduce administration page:

Map Task Capacity	Reduce Task Capacity
3	3

The following screenshot shows partial job details where you can find the **Num Tasks** and **Running** Hadoop counters. You will learn how to set these values correctly later in this chapter.

Kind	% Complete	Num Tasks	Pending	Running	Complete	Killed	Failed/Killed Task Attempts
map	100.00%	16	0	0	16	0	0 / 0
reduce	100.00%	3	0	0	3	0	0 / 0

Checking for CPU contention

Nowadays, all operating systems are multitasking systems and utilize multicore CPUs. In order to allow multitasking and enable multiple processes to share a single CPU, the operating system needs to store and restore the CPU state (context) when switching between processes, so that execution can be resumed from the same point at a later time. This is what is called **Context Switch**. The operating system assigns a priority for each task that will be executed by the CPU. Contention occurs when all lower priority tasks wait when any higher priority CPU-bound task is running and there are no other CPUs that can handle other tasks. Consequently, when the number of Context Switches per second is high, it means that the CPU is busy and is spending a lot of time storing and restoring process states.

Therefore, excessive context switching means that you're possibly running too many tasks on your host. When configuring MapReduce, as a rule of thumb, the total of `mapred.tasktracker.map.tasks.maximum` and `mapred.tasktracker.reduce.tasks.maximum` should be around the total CPU's cores, that is, 1 in a normal condition or 120 to 150 percent of the logical cores on your host. Due to Hyper-Threading, the CPU might process more than one job at a time.

In order to display the Context Switch's statistics, you may use the `vmstat` Linux tool, which is very helpful to display utilization statistics of your CPU (**cs** = Context Switch).

The following screenshot shows the `vmstat` output on a lightly used machine. The **in** column indicates the number of interrupts per second. If this number is high (*value* * *1000* or more), it indicates a heavily used machine or problem with the hardware.

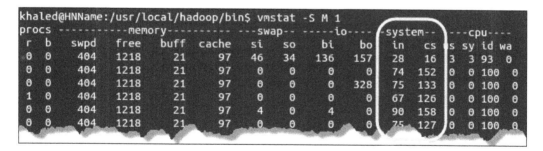

The `vmstat` tool was launched using the `-S M 1` command. The `-S` parameter is used to set the unit size, M indicates the unit size: 1048576, and the last parameter 1 indicates the delay between updates.

The following screenshot shows the `vmstat` output on a heavily used machine. You can observe that the number of interrupts per second (the **in** column) is high in comparison to the lightly used machine.

```
khaled@HNName:~$ vmstat -S M 1
procs ----------memory---------- ---swap-- -----io---- -system-- ----cpu----
 r  b   swpd   free   buff  cache   si   so    bi    bo   in   cs us sy id wa
 7  2   1353     58      0    57    33    27   105   140   17  102  3  3 94  0
 0 14   1360     57      0    63  2192  8072  3784 46456 2687 6515 25 39  2 34
 6  1   1360     64      0    56  4480  1260  7044 13492 2527 5547 18 22  8 51
 2  3   1358    884      2    72  6252   480 19308   504 3649 7354 24 38 10 28
 5  0   1358    840      2    80   236     0  8720     0 2265 3653 40 14  9 37
 7  1   1358    797      2    85   232     0  5888     0 2053 2993 58 14  6 22
 8  4   1358    755      2    88   640     0  3736   460 1525 1764 87 10  1  2
 3  3   1358    737      2    92   248     0  4024     0 1695 1799 85 11  2  2
```

Sizing your Hadoop cluster

As discussed earlier, Hadoop's performance depends on multiple factors based on well-configured software layers and well-dimensioned hardware resources that utilize its CPU, Memory, hard drive (storage I/O) and network bandwidth efficiently.

Planning the Hadoop cluster remains a complex task that requires minimum knowledge of the Hadoop architecture and may be out the scope of this book. This is what we are trying to make clearer in this section by providing explanations and formulas in order to help you to best estimate your needs. We will introduce a basic guideline that will help you to make your decision while sizing your cluster and answer some *How to plan* questions about cluster's needs such as the following:

- How to plan my storage?
- How to plan my CPU?
- How to plan my memory?
- How to plan the network bandwidth?

While sizing your Hadoop cluster, you should also consider the data volume that the final users will process on the cluster. The answer to this question will lead you to determine how many machines (nodes) you need in your cluster to process the input data efficiently and determine the disk/memory capacity of each one.

Hadoop is a Master/Slave architecture and needs a lot of memory and CPU bound. It has two main components:

- **JobTracker**: This is the critical component in this architecture and monitors jobs that are running on the cluster
- **TaskTracker**: This runs tasks on each node of the cluster

To work efficiently, HDFS must have high throughput hard drives with an underlying filesystem that supports the HDFS read and write pattern (large block). This pattern defines one big read (or write) at a time with a block size of 64 MB, 128 MB, up to 256 MB. Also, the network layer should be fast enough to cope with intermediate data transfer and block.

HDFS is itself based on a Master/Slave architecture with two main components: the NameNode / Secondary NameNode and DataNode components. These are critical components and need a lot of memory to store the file's meta information such as attributes and file localization, directory structure, names, and to process data. The NameNode component ensures that data blocks are properly replicated in the cluster. The second component, the DataNode component, manages the state of an HDFS node and interacts with its data blocks. It requires a lot of I/O for processing and data transfer.

Typically, the MapReduce layer has two main prerequisites: input datasets must be large enough to fill a data block and split in smaller and independent data chunks (for example, a 10 GB text file can be split into 40,960 blocks of 256 MB each, and each line of text in any data block can be processed independently). The second prerequisite is that it should consider the **data locality**, which means that the MapReduce code is moved where the data lies, not the opposite (it is more efficient to move a few megabytes of code to be close to the data to be processed, than moving many data blocks over the network or the disk). This involves having a distributed storage system that exposes data locality and allows the execution of code on any storage node.

Concerning the network bandwidth, it is used at two instances: during the replication process and following a file write, and during the balancing of the replication factor when a node fails.

The most common practice to size a Hadoop cluster is sizing the cluster based on the amount of storage required. The more data into the system, the more will be the machines required. Each time you add a new node to the cluster, you get more computing resources in addition to the new storage capacity.

Let's consider an example cluster growth plan based on storage and learn how to determine the storage needed, the amount of memory, and the number of DataNodes in the cluster.

Daily data input	100 GB	*Storage space used by daily data input = daily data input * replication factor = 300 GB*
HDFS replication factor	3	
Monthly growth	5%	*Monthly volume = (300 * 30) + 5% = 9450 GB*
		*After one year = 9450 * (1 + 0.05)^12 = 16971 GB*
Intermediate MapReduce data	25%	*Dedicated space = HDD size * (1 – Non HDFS reserved space per disk / 100 + Intermediate MapReduce data / 100)*
Non HDFS reserved space per disk	30%	*= 4 * (1 – (0.25 + 0.30)) = 1.8 TB (which is the node capacity)*
Size of a hard drive disk	4 TB	
Number of DataNodes needed to process:		
Whole first month data = 9.450 / 1800 ~= 6 nodes		
The 12th month data = 16.971/ 1800 ~= 10 nodes		
Whole year data = 157.938 / 1800 ~= 88 nodes		

Do not use RAID array disks on a DataNode. HDFS provides its own replication mechanism. It is also important to note that for every disk, 30 percent of its capacity should be reserved to non-HDFS use.

It is easy to determine the memory needed for both NameNode and Secondary NameNode. The memory needed by NameNode to manage the HDFS cluster metadata in memory and the memory needed for the OS must be added together. Typically, the memory needed by Secondary NameNode should be identical to NameNode. Then you can apply the following formulas to determine the memory amount:

NameNode memory	2 GB – 4 GB	*Memory amount = HDFS cluster management memory + NameNode memory + OS memory*
Secondary NameNode memory	2 GB – 4 GB	
OS memory	4 GB – 8 GB	
HDFS memory	2 GB – 8 GB	
At least NameNode (Secondary NameNode) memory = 2 + 2 + 4 = 8 GB		

It is also easy to determine the DataNode memory amount. However, this time, the memory amount depends on the physical CPU's core number installed on each DataNode.

DataNode process memory	4 GB – 8 GB	*Memory amount = Memory per CPU core * number of CPU's core + DataNode process memory + DataNode TaskTracker memory + OS memory*
DataNode TaskTracker memory	4 GB – 8 GB	
OS memory	4 GB – 8 GB	
CPU's core number	4+	
Memory per CPU core	4 GB – 8 GB	
At least DataNode memory = 4*4 + 4 + 4 + 4 = 28 GB		

Regarding how to determine the CPU and the network bandwidth, we suggest using the now-a-days multicore CPUs with at least four physical cores per CPU. The more physical CPU's cores you have, the more you will be able to enhance your job's performance (according to all rules discussed to avoid underutilization or overutilization). For the network switches, we recommend to use an equipment having a high throughput (such as 10 GB) Ethernet intra rack with N x 10 GB Ethernet inter rack.

Configuring your cluster correctly

To run Hadoop and get a maximum performance, it needs to be configured correctly. But the question is how to do that. Well, based on our experiences, we can say that there is not one single answer to this question. The experiences gave us a clear indication that the Hadoop framework should be adapted for the cluster it is running on and sometimes also to the job.

In order to configure your cluster correctly, we recommend running a Hadoop job(s) the first time with its default configuration to get a baseline (see *Chapter 3, Detecting System Bottlenecks*). Then, you will check the resource's weakness (if it exists) by analyzing the job history logfiles and report the results (measured time it took to run the jobs). After that, iteratively, you will tune your Hadoop configuration and re-run the job until you get the configuration that fits your business needs.

The number of mappers and reducer tasks that a job should use is important. Picking the right amount of tasks for a job can have a huge impact on Hadoop's performance.

The number of reducer tasks should be less than the number of mapper tasks. Google reports one reducer for 20 mappers; the others give different guidelines. This is because mapper tasks often process a lot of data, and the result of those tasks are passed to the reducer tasks. Often, a reducer task is just an aggregate function that processes a minor portion of the data compared to the mapper tasks. Also, the correct number of reducers must also be considered.

The number of mappers and reducers is related to the number of physical cores on the DataNode, which determines the maximum number of jobs that can run in parallel on DataNode.

In a Hadoop cluster, **master** nodes typically consist of machines where one machine is designed as a NameNode, and another as a JobTracker, while all other machines in the cluster are slave nodes that act as DataNodes and TaskTrackers. When starting the cluster, you begin starting the HDFS daemons on the master node and DataNode daemons on all data nodes machines. Then, you start the MapReduce daemons: JobTracker on the master node and the TaskTracker daemons on all slave nodes. The following diagram shows the Hadoop daemon's pseudo formula:

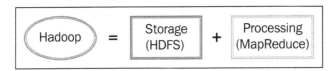

When configuring your cluster, you need to consider the CPU cores and memory resources that need to be allocated to these daemons. In a huge data context, it is recommended to reserve 2 CPU cores on each DataNode for the HDFS and MapReduce daemons. While in a small and medium data context, you can reserve only one CPU core on each DataNode.

Once you have determined the maximum mapper's slot numbers, you need to determine the reducer's maximum slot numbers. Based on our experience, there is a distribution between the Map and Reduce tasks on DataNodes that give good performance result to define the reducer's slot numbers the same as the mapper's slot numbers or at least equal to two-third mapper slots.

Let's learn to correctly configure the number of mappers and reducers and assume the following cluster examples:

Cluster machine	Nb	Medium data size	Large data size
DataNode CPU cores	8	Reserve 1 CPU core	Reserve 2 CPU cores
DataNode TaskTracker daemon	1	1	1

Cluster machine	Nb	Medium data size	Large data size
DataNode HDFS daemon	1	1	1
Data block size		128 MB	256 MB
DataNode CPU % utilization		95% to 120%	95% to 150%
Cluster nodes		20	40
Replication factor		2	3

We want to use the CPU resources at least 95 percent, and due to Hyper-Threading, one CPU core might process more than one job at a time, so we can set the Hyper-Threading factor range between 120 percent and 170 percent.

Maximum mapper's slot numbers on one node in a large data context	= *number of physical cores – reserved core * (0.95 -> 1.5)* *Reserved core = 1 for TaskTracker + 1 for HDFS*
Let's say the CPU on the node will use up to 120% (with Hyper-Threading): *Maximum number of mapper slots = (8 – 2) * 1.2 = 7.2 rounded down to 7*	
Let's apply the 2/3 mappers / reducers technique: *Maximum number of reducers slots = 7 * 2/3 = 5*	
Let's define the number of slots for the cluster: *Mapper's slots: = 7 * 40 = 280* *Reducer's slots: = 5 * 40 = 200*	

The block size (discussed in *Chapter 2, An Overview of the Hadoop Parameters*) is also used to enhance performance. The default Hadoop configuration uses 64 MB blocks, while we suggest using 128 MB in your configuration for a medium data context as well and 256 MB for a very large data context. This means that a mapper task can process one data block (for example, 128 MB) by only opening one block. In the default Hadoop configuration (set to 2 by default), two mapper tasks are needed to process the same amount of data. This may be considered as a drawback because initializing one more mapper task and opening one more file takes more time.

Summary

In this chapter, we introduced some scenarios and techniques that may help you to identify your cluster's weakness. You learned how to check your Hadoop cluster node's health and how to identify a massive I/O traffic. Also, we talked about how to identify CPU contention using the `vmstat` Linux tool.

Then we learned some formulas that you need to use in order to size your Hadoop cluster correctly. Also, in the last section, you learned how to configure the number of mappers and reducers correctly using a new, dedicated formula.

In the next chapter, you will learn more about profiling map and reduce tasks, and will dive more deeply in to the universe of Hadoop map and reduce tasks.

5
Enhancing Map and Reduce Tasks

The Hadoop framework already includes several counters such as the number of bytes read and written. These counters are very helpful to learn about the framework activities and the resources used. These counters are sent by the worker nodes to the master nodes periodically.

In this chapter, for both map and reduce, we will learn how to enhance each phase, what counters to look at, and the techniques to apply in order to analyze a performance issue. Then, you will learn how to tune the correct configuration parameter with the appropriate value.

In this chapter, we will cover the following topics:

- The impact of the block size and input data
- How to deal with small and unsplittable files
- Reducing map-side spilling records
- Improving the Reduce phase
- Calculating Map and Reduce tasks' throughput
- Tuning map and reduce parameters

Enhancing map tasks

When executing a MapReduce job, the Hadoop framework will execute the job in a well-defined sequence of processing phases. Except the user-defined functions (map, reduce, and combiner), the execution time of other MapReduce phases are generic across different MapReduce jobs. The processing time mainly depends on the amount of data flowing through each phase and the performance of the underlying Hadoop cluster.

In order to enhance MapReduce performance, you first need to benchmark these different phases by running a set of different jobs with different amounts of data (per map/reduce tasks). Running these jobs is needed to collect measurements such as durations and data amount for each phase, and then analyze these measurements (for each of the phases) to derive the platform scaling functions.

To identify map-side bottlenecks, you should outline five phases of the map task execution flow. The following figure represents the map tasks' execution sequence:

Let us see what each stage does:

- During the **Read** phase, a map task typically reads a block with a fixed size (for example, 64 MB) from the **Hadoop Distributed File System** (HDFS). However, written data files are different and might be of arbitrary size, for example, 80 MB. In this case, to store the data, there will be two blocks: one of 64 MB and the other of 16 MB. When profiling this phase, we will measure the duration of the **Read** phase as well as the amount of data read by the map task.

- To profile the **Map** phase, you need to measure the duration of the entire map function and the number of processed records and then normalize this execution time per record. When measuring the execution time, you should check for any skewed data, which is often the result of large number of small input files or a large unsplittable file. You should compare input sizes across all map tasks (for the same job), to check whether there is any skewed data.

- During the **Spill** phase, the framework locally sorts the intermediate data and partitions it for the different reduce tasks, applies the combiner if available, and then writes the intermediate data to the local disk. To profile this phase, we will measure the time taken to do all of this. If you are using Combiners (discussed in *Chapter 6, Optimizing MapReduce Tasks*), the processing time will include their execution time.

- In the **Fetch** phase, we will measure the time taken by the framework to buffer map phase outputs into memory as well as the amount of generated intermediate data. In the last phase, that is the **Merge** phase, we will measure the time that the framework took for merging different spill files into a single spill file for each reduce task.

Input data and block size impact

Prior to the read phase, data should be located on the filesystem. Your data scheme will also affect your MapReduce job performance. To run a map task efficiently, data must be splittable, such as text files, so that MapReduce can break tasks into chunks and process each one independently. A split file should be big enough to fill one block size. The block size is important because it determines how your data is split up and every input split will be assigned to a mapper. Therefore, if you have a very large dataset but a small block size, this can result in a lot of mappers. This means mappers will finish very fast but will take time to split up and finish. So, for a large input file, this value should be high (for example, 256 MB). Default Hadoop block sizes are 64 MB (good choice for small dataset), 128 MB (for medium dataset), and 256 MB (for large dataset). A larger block size may speed disk I/O but would increase the transfer of data across the network and may also cause spilled records during the map phase.

A map task has two ways to read data from storage systems, directly from the disk (direct I/O) or by streaming the data (streaming I/O from the storage system by an interprocess communication scheme such as TCP/IP or JDBC), which is more general and can be used for reading data from both the local node and the remote node.

Hadoop distributes data to multiple nodes to balance the cluster's workload and assigns tasks to computing nodes where input data is located. This is why data locality is important and may impact the performance of the cluster. If the data is not located on the node where the mapper will process it, data will be transferred across the network, which will increase network traffic. Direct I/O is more efficient if the map function reads data from the local node (data-local maps). The Streaming I/O is the only choice if a map function is not a data-local map.

Dealing with small and unsplittable files

Your business may require that you process large and small, binary or compressed files that HDFS can't split. Binary and compressed files are by nature not block-based. Therefore, this may affect the performance of your MapReduce jobs due to the loss of data locality.

Hadoop was not designed to deal with small files, and the HDFS is designed to store and process large datasets (terabytes). However, storing a large number of small files in HDFS is inefficient. The problem with a large number of small files is there will be a lot of parallel tasks to process these files, and too much parallelism can consume more resources than necessary, which will impact the runtime of your job. Also, in the case of large number of small files stored in the system, their metadata occupies a large portion of the system, which is limited by the NameNode physical memory capacities.

A split file is considered to be small if its size is less than the HDFS block size (by default 64 MB), and big if its size exceeds the block size. In order to inspect the size of your input files, browse the Hadoop DFS Home at `http://machinename:50070/dfshealth.jsp` and click on **Browse the filesystem**. The following screenshot shows a DFS directory that contains small files; each file has a size of 1 MB and a block size of 256 MB:

Go to parent directory

Name	Type	Size	Replication	Block Size	Modificati
test_io_0	file	1 MB	2	256 MB	2013-11-
test_io_1	file	1 MB	2	256 MB	2013-11
test_io_10	file	1 MB	2	256 MB	2013-11-
test_io_11	file	1 MB	2	256 MB	2013-11
test_io_12	file	1 MB	2	256 MB	2013-11-
test_io_13	file	1 MB	2	256 MB	2013-11
test_io_14	file	1 MB	2	256 MB	2013-11-
test_io_15	file	1 MB	2	256 MB	2013-11-

The easiest way to solve the problem of HDFS small files with Hadoop is to work to package them into a larger file. In this case, you store less files in the NameNode memory and improve data interchange, and all your small files will be stored on the local disk in a single file. In order to pack small files when using Hadoop, you can choose any of the following alternatives:

- Create container files using Avro to serialize data. Avro is an Apache open source project (`http://avro.apache.org/`) that provides data serialization for Hadoop and data exchange services, which can be used together or independently.

- Use Hadoop Archives (HAR files). The HAR files are special format archives and work by building a layered filesystem on top of HDFS so that the original files can be accessed in parallel, in a transparent manner, and efficiently by Hadoop without expanding the files. To create a HAR file archive, you can use the `hadoop archive` command and use a `har://` URL to access the files.

- Use a sequence file (SequenceFile) to store small files into one larger single file. SequenceFile is structured the same way as a key/value pair in which you define the filename as a key and its contents as the value. Another advantage of using sequence file is that such files are splittable and allow block compression.

To determine whether a file will fit into a block, you need to calculate the average number of input bytes for each map task and compare it to the block size. In case you find the average larger than the block size, then you need to investigate why Hadoop didn't split your file. This may be because your file is not compliant with the TextInputFormat or LzoTextInputFormat interface.

 Hadoop compression codecs such as Deflate, gzip, lzo, and Snappy are not splittable.

Reducing spilled records during the Map phase

Map functions may write a large amount of data to the local filesystem during the map phase. While Map tasks are running, they generate intermediate data output which is stored into a memory buffer that is set to 100 MB by default (io.sort.mb). This buffer is a chunk of reserved memory that is part of the Map JVM heap space. As soon as a threshold of occupancy is reached (io.sort.spill.percent), the content of the buffer is flushed to the local disk, this is what we call **spill**. To store the spilled records' metadata (length of 16-bytes for each record), the Hadoop framework allocates 0.05 percent of the memory allocated by io.sort.mb (parameter, io.sort.record.percent) and hence 5 MB is allocated to the metadata and 95 MB is left for buffer use. Take a look at the following diagram:

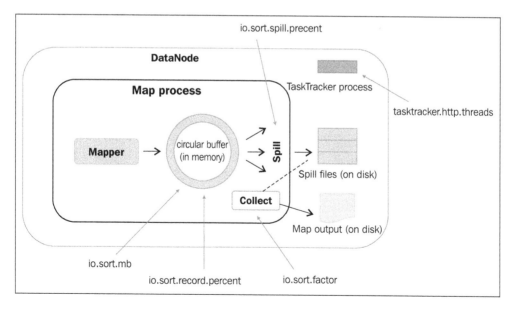

Each of the parameters shown in the preceding diagram are described in the following table:

Parameter	Default value	Tuning recommendation
`io.sort.mb`	100	This parameter indicates the amount of memory in megabytes allocated to sort and store the map task's output. To set this value, it is good practice to not exceed 70 to 75 percent of one-fifth of the available memory on the DataNode.
`io.sort.factor`	10	This sort factor parameter indicates the number of files to merge together in a single pass. Depending on your DataNode memory size, this value should be set to one-tenth of the amount of memory defined by `io.sort.mb`.
`io.sort.record.percent`	0.05	This parameter determines the percentage of `io.sort.mb` used to store map output's metadata. We recommend to keep the default value for this parameter.
`io.sort.spill.percent`	0.80	This parameter determines the percentage of the map output buffer after which the buffer will be spilled to the disk. We recommend that you keep the default value for this parameter. To nearly use the full buffer capacity, you can set the value up to `0.99`.
`tasktrakker.http.threads`	40	This parameter determines the number of threads that serve mappers' output to reducers. This value is set per tracker and should not be set by individual jobs. This value may be increased on a very large cluster.

Performance issues and reading overhead may occur when spilling records to the disk multiple times. Profiling these MapReduce data flow steps means to detect whether your map task is performing additional spills. To determine whether there are additional spills, you should compare **Map output records** and **Spilled Records** Hadoop counters, and if the number of **Spilled Records** is greater than **Map output records**, it is certain that additional spilling is occurring. The following screenshot reports Hadoop counters for a MapReduce job that has spilled records:

Map-Reduce Framework

Map output materialized bytes	68,451,096
Map input records	671,089
Spilled Records	1,342,178
Map output bytes	67,108,900
Total committed heap usage (bytes)	260,046,848
CPU time spent (ms)	15,420
Map input bytes	67,108,900
SPLIT_RAW_BYTES	94
Combine input records	0
Combine output records	0
Physical memory (bytes) snapshot	158,150,656
Virtual memory (bytes) snapshot	1,169,850,368
Map output records	671,089

To enhance the framework's performance at this stage and eliminate the additional spills to disk, you need to allocate the memory buffer with an accurate value and set the `io.sort.spill.percent` to `0.99` to use nearly the full buffer capacity.

To determine the memory space required by the buffer, you should calculate the total size of the buffer (records + metadata). To calculate `io.sort.record.percent` and `io.sort.mb`, you need to calculate the following values (let's assume that we use reported counters from the previous screenshot):

- **Record length** (**RL**) = map output bytes / map output records, that is, 671,089,000 / 6,710,890 = 100 bytes

- **Spilled Records size** (**RS**) = Spilled Records number * Record length, that is, 1,342,178 * 100 = 134,217,800 bytes = 128 MB

- **Metadata size** (**MS**) = metadata length * Spilled Records number, that is, 1,342,178 * 16 = 21,474,848 bytes = 20.48 MB

Once you have calculated the values of RL, RS, and MS, you may now calculate the total size of the buffer (records + metadata) as follows:

- `io.sort.record.percent` = metadata length / (metadata length + Record length), that is, 16 / (16 + 100) = 0.138

- `io.sort.mb` = Metadata size + Spilled Records size, that is, 128 + 20.48 ≈ 149 MB

Calculating map tasks' throughput

During the Map phase, a map task may be slowed by small files, which means Hadoop is spending a lot of time to start and stop tasks. When working with large unsplittable files, Hadoop spends I/O time reading data from the other node. Also poor read/write disk operations will affect Hadoop's MapReduce performance.

To determine whether your map tasks run slowly and have a low throughput, you need to calculate this throughput using the Hadoop I/O counters based on the file size written (or read) by the individual map tasks and the elapsed time to process the job. Then, if the calculated throughput is close to the local I/O throughput, you can consider it as the optimal throughput, otherwise, some other factor is affecting your map tasks' performance.

Let's assume you have a MapReduce job using N map tasks; the throughput is calculated in bytes/sec (bytes per second) as follows:

Throughput (N map tasks) = sum (each map input size in bytes) / sum (each map execution time in seconds).

The following screenshot shows the Hadoop counter you need to calculate the map task's throughput, which you can find on the task stats history:

Map-Reduce Framework	
Map output materialized bytes	68,451,096
Map input records	671,089
Spilled Records	1,342,178
Map output bytes	67,108,900
Total committed heap usage (bytes)	260,046,848
CPU time spent (ms)	15,420
Map input bytes	67,108,900
SPLIT_RAW_BYTES	94
Combine input records	0
Combine output records	0
Physical memory (bytes) snapshot	158,150,656
Virtual memory (bytes) snapshot	1,169,850,368
Map output records	671,089

The reported map execution time is shown in the following screenshot:

Task Id	Start Time	Finish Time
attempt_201311141600_0001_m_000000_0	14/11 18:12:39	14/11 18:13:03 (24sec)

Therefore, by using the counter's values for this single sample map task, the throughput is, *67,108,900 / 24 = 2,796,204.16 ≈ 2,66 MB/sec.*

It is recommended to determine map task's performance throughput based on the average map tasks' throughput and not on one map's throughput, unless your job uses only one map task. You can calculate the average map tasks' throughput using the formula *average throughput = sum (each map input size in bytes / time in seconds) / number of map tasks.*

It is also interesting to calculate the concurrent average throughput in order to determine your cluster capabilities. Let's say you have a cluster with a capacity of 100 map slots, 5.231 MB/s I/O throughput, 4.863 MB/s average I/O throughput, and you want to process 5000 files (256 MB each). In this case, because of the cluster capacity, this job will be processed in 50 MapReduce waves (*5000 / 100 = 50*). To calculate the concurrent throughput, multiply the throughput rate by the minimum of the number of files (5000 in this example) and the number of available map slots in your cluster (100 in this example).

In our example, you can calculate the concurrent throughput as *5.231 * 100 = 523.1 MB/s*. The average concurrent throughput can be calculated as *4.863 * 100 = 486.3 MB/s*.

Calculating the average concurrent throughput will help you to estimate the time required to process your input files using your Hadoop cluster. Therefore, in our example, 5000 files will be processed in *(5000 files * 256 MB each) / 486.3 MB/s average throughput = 2632.12 sec ≈ 44 min.*

Enhancing reduce tasks

Reduce task processing consists of a sequence of three phases. Only the execution of the user-defined reduce function is custom, and its duration depends on the amount of data flowing through each phase and the performance of the underlying Hadoop cluster. Profiling each of these phases will help you to identify potential bottlenecks and low speeds of data processing. The following figure shows the three major phases of Reduce tasks:

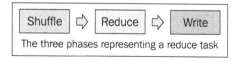

The three phases representing a reduce task

Let's see each phase in some detail:

- Profiling the **Shuffle** phase implies that you need to measure the time taken to transfer the intermediate data from map tasks to the reduce tasks and then merge and sort them together. In the shuffle phase, the intermediate data generated by the map phase is fetched. The processing time of this phase significantly depends on Hadoop configuration parameters and the amount of intermediate data that is destined for the reduce task.

- In the **Reduce** phase, each reduce task is assigned a partition of the map output intermediate data with a fixed key range; so the reduce task must fetch the content of this partition from every map task's output in the cluster. The execution time is the time taken to apply the user-supplied reduce function on the input key and all the values corresponding to it. To profile the Reduce phase, measure the execution time, which also depends on the size of the input data.

- Profiling the **Write** phase, which is the last phase, means measuring how long Hadoop takes to write the reduce output to HDFS.

Calculating reduce tasks' throughput

On the reduce-side, reduction in speed may be caused by a bad or nonoptimized reduce function user code, hardware issue, or a misconfiguration of the Hadoop framework. To determine the throughput of your reduce tasks, you can calculate this throughput using the Hadoop I/O counters (as you did for the map tasks' throughput).

For a given MapReduce job using N reduce tasks, the throughput is calculated in bytes/sec (bytes per second) using the formula *throughput (N reduce tasks) = sum (each reduce input shuffle in bytes) / sum (each reduce execution time in seconds)*.

The following screenshot shows the Hadoop counter you need to calculate the reduce tasks' throughput:

Map-Reduce Framework	
Reduce input groups	3,504,010
Combine output records	0
Reduce shuffle bytes	357,409,116
Physical memory (bytes) snapshot	349,847,552
Reduce output records	3,504,010
Spilled Records	3,504,010
Total committed heap usage (bytes)	325,058,560
CPU time spent (ms)	48,400
Virtual memory (bytes) snapshot	1,181,282,304
Combine input records	0
Reduce input records	3,504,010

The following screenshot shows the `reduce` function's execution time:

Shuffle Finished	Sort Finished	Finish Time
14/11 18:15:40 (2mins, 36sec)	14/11 18:15:40 (0sec)	14/11 18:16:06 (3mins, 2sec)

The Reduce phase's total execution time is the aggregation of the execution time of three steps: the Shuffle execution time, the Sort time, and the Reduce function execution time. The execution time for each step is reported by Hadoop logs, as shown in the previous screenshot.

It may also be interesting to calculate the Shuffle and Sort steps' throughputs. You can calculate the Shuffle throughput by dividing the Shuffle bytes by the Shuffle execution time (in seconds). Also, to calculate the Sort step throughput, you need to divide the Shuffle bytes by the Sort execution time (in seconds). The *Shuffle throughput* is calculated as *Shuffle bytes / Shuffle time* and *Sort throughput* as *Shuffle bytes / Sort time*.

As you can see, these formulas may lead to a division by zero error if the Shuffle or Sort time is equal to zero. The Shuffle and Sort throughputs are inversely proportional to the Shuffle and Sort time. This means, the closer the Shuffle or Sort time is to zero, the bigger will be the Shuffle or Sort throughput, which means the throughput is maximum at lowest Shuffle or Sort time values.

Improving Reduce execution phase

Once map tasks have processed data, the map output data shuffled at different times needs to be merged to a single reduce input file and sorted by a key before a reduce task can use it. The size of a map output depends on the size of its input dataset. The easiest way to enhance performance in the Shuffle and Sort phases is to reduce the amount of data to be sorted and merged. This is typically done by using combiners, data compression, and/or data filtering. (Using combiners and implementing compression is discussed in *Chapter 6, Optimizing MapReduce Tasks*.)

Local disk issues and network problems are common sources of performance issues in the Shuffle and Sort phases as the MapReduce framework reads the spilled local inputs and feeds them to the reduce code.

Within the Reduce phase, a high volume of traffic network is usually observed due to the data transfer between Map and Reduce tasks. Hadoop has several configuration parameters that you can tune in order to enhance its performance in this phase. The following table shows the common parameters tuned to enhance the Reduce phase:

Parameter	Default value	Tuning recommendation
mapred.reduce.parallel.copies	5	This parameter controls the number of threads in the Reducer task.
io.sort.factor	10	This sort factor parameter indicates the number of files to merge together in a single pass. Depending on your DataNode memory size, this value should be set to one-tenth of the amount of memory defined by io.sort.mb.
mapred.job.reduce.input.buffer.percent	0.0	This parameter determines the percentage of memory — relative to the maximum memory heap size — to retain map outputs during the reduce phase.
mapred.job.shuffle.input.buffer.percent	0.7	This parameter determines the percentage of memory to be allocated from the maximum memory heap size to storing map outputs during the shuffle phase.

By setting mapred.job.reduce.input.buffer.percent value to 0.8, the buffer will be used up to 80 percent, which will keep the reducer input data in memory. Because the default value 0.0 means that map outputs are merged into the local disk rather than in memory.

It is also recommended to maximize the memory allocated to store map output during the Shuffle phase. Therefore, you can increase the mapred.job.shuffle.input.buffer.percent value up to 0.9 to use 90 percent of the memory heap size rather than 70 percent of the default size.

Tuning map and reduce parameters

Picking the right amount of tasks for a job can have a huge impact on Hadoop's performance. In *Chapter 4*, *Identifying Resource Weaknesses*, you learned how to configure the number of mappers and reducers correctly. But sizing the number of mappers and reducers correctly is not enough to get the maximum performance of a MapReduce job. The optimum occurs when every machine in the cluster has something to do at any given time when a job is executed. Remember that Hadoop framework has more than 180 parameters and most of them should not keep their default settings.

In this section, we will present other techniques to calculate your mappers' and reducers' numbers. It may be more productive to try more than one optimization method, because we aim to find a particular configuration for a given job that uses all available resources on your cluster. The outcome of this change is to enable the user to run as many mappers and reducers in parallel as possible to fully utilize the available resources.

The theoretical upper bound limit of your mappers can be calculated by dividing the input file size by the block size. On the other hand, your input file is processed by machines with a fixed number of CPU cores (*#mappers = number of physical cores - reserved core * (0.95 to 1.75)*). This means to process a 10 GB file on a cluster of three nodes each with eight CPU cores and a 256 MB block size, the mappers optimal number is somewhere between 37 and 40. The upper limit of mappers is 10 GB / 0.25 GB = 40. The mappers optimal number can be calculated as follows:

- *#mappers based on CPU core number = (8 cores - 1 reserved cores) * 1.75 = 12.25*
- *#cluster mappers capacity = 12.25 * 3 = 37.5*

There are different techniques that you can use to determine the number of mappers and reducers accurately. All these techniques are based on calculations and tuned or adjusted according to real-world experiences. You should not focus on just one technique, but try each one of these techniques in your own environment to find the one that lets your cluster run optimally.

In *Chapter 3*, *Detecting System Bottlenecks*, we suggest to set the reducer's number between 50 percent and 99 percent of the cluster capacity so that all the reducers finish in one wave. This technique suggests that you calculate the reducers number using this formula: *(0.5 to 0.95) * nodes number * reducers slots number*.

In *Chapter 4*, *Identifying Resource Weaknesses*, we suggest setting the number of reducers' slots the same as the mappers' slots or at least to two-thirds of the mappers. Experience shows that this calculation technique is an easy and fast way to set the reducers' numbers on small cluster size or development environment.

To determine the lower bounds of your reducer's number, you should divide the CPU cores' number per node by two (*(cores per node) / 2*). To determine the upper bound, you multiply the CPU cores' number by two, (*2 * (cores per node)*). You can also use the two-thirds mappers' technique to specify the reducers' number in this range.

In this section, we will suggest two formulas to determine the mappers' and reducers' numbers based on the number of your cluster nodes and CPU cores. You can use these formulas as a starting point to calculate these numbers and then fine-tune them in your environment to get the optimal values as follows:

- Use the cluster nodes' number to calculate the number of mappers and reducers using the formula *number of reducers = (0.95 to 1.75) * (number of nodes * mapred.reduce.parallel.copies)*. Here, 0.95 to 1.75 is the CPU hyperthreading factor and `mapred.reduce.parallel.copies` is the configuration parameter that determines the maximum number of reducers that can run in parallel.

- Use the CPU cores' number to calculate the number of mappers and reducers using the formula *number of reducers = (0.95 to 1.75) * (number of CPU cores - 1)*.

Let's return to our cluster example (three nodes, each node has one CPU * four cores, 4 GB RAM, and 40 GB HDD space, which we used to create the baseline in *Chapter 3, Detecting System Bottlenecks*). The following table summarizes the different calculation techniques:

Calculation technique	Formula to use	#mappers	#reducers
Set the reducers' number between 50 percent and 99 percent of the cluster	*#mappers = CPU cores - 1 * 1.75* *#reducers = (0.5 to 0.95) * nodes number * reducers' slots number*	4 - 1 * 1.75 = 5	0.95 * 3 * 5 = 14.25 ≈ 14
Determine reducers' upper and lower bounds	*#mappers = CPU cores - 1 * 1.75* *#reducers LB = (cores per node) / 2* *#reducers UB = 2 * (cores per node)* *If you apply the 2/3 mappers technique: =5*2/3 = 3.33 ≈ 3 (which is in the range)*	5	LB = 4/2 = 2 UB = 2*4= 8
Based on node numbers	*#mappers = CPU cores - 1 * 1.75* *#reducers = 1.75 * (number of nodes * mapred.reduce.parallel.copies)*	5	1.75 * (3 * 5) = 26.25 ≈ 25
Based on CPU cores	*#mappers = CPU cores - 1 * 1.75* *#reducers = (0.95 to 1.75) * (number of CPU cores -1)*	5	1.75 * 3 = 5.25 ≈ 5

We applied the third and fourth technique's calculation results to the test cluster environment and the reported result in Tuned 2 and Tuned 3 columns in the following table (Baseline and Tuned 1 columns are reported from *Chapter 3, Detecting System Bottlenecks*). In comparison to the Tuned 1 column, we will use a larger block size (256 MB, 128 MB in the previous iteration) and allocate more memory (-Xmx550m) using the `mapred.child.java.opts` parameter:

Hadoop parameter	Baseline	Tuned 1	Tuned 2	Tuned 2
dfs.replication	3	2	2	2
dfs.block.size	6,7108,864	134,217,728	268,435,456	268,435,456
dfs.namenode.handler.count	10	20	20	20
dfs.datanode.handler.count	3	5	5	5
io.sort.factor	10	35	35	35
io.sort.mb	100	350	350	350
mapred.tasktracker.map.tasks.maximum	2	5	5	5
mapred.map.tasks	2	2	2	2
mapred.reduce.tasks	1	8	26	5
mapred.tasktracker.reduce.tasks.maximum	2	5	5	5
mapred.reduce.parallel.copies	5	5	5	5
mapred.job.reduce.input.buffer.percent	0	0	0	0
mapred.child.java.opts	-Xmx200m	-Xmx500m	-Xmx550m	-Xmx550m
Input data size	10 GB	10 GB	10 GB	10 GB
Cluster's nodes number	3	3	3	3
Job execution time (sec)	243	185	169	190
Improvement over Baseline (%)		23.86%	30.45%	21.81%

These jobs are all done on a test environment using autogenerated data. You may get different results when trying these techniques on your cluster.

Summary

In this chapter, we learned about map-side and reduce-side tasks' enhancement and introduced some techniques that may help you to improve the performance of your MapReduce job. We learned how important the impact of the block size is and how to identify slow map-side performance due to small and unsplittable files. Also, we learned about spilling files and how to eliminate them by allocating an accurate amount of memory buffer.

Then, we moved ahead and learned how to identify a low performance job within the Shuffle and Merge steps during the Reduce phase. In the last section, we covered different techniques to calculate mappers' and reducers' numbers to tune your MapReduce configuration and enhance its performance.

In the next chapter, we will learn more about the optimization of MapReduce task and take a look at how combiners and intermediate data compression will enhance the MapReduce job performance. Keep reading!

Optimizing MapReduce Tasks

6

Most MapReduce programs are written for data analysis and they usually take a lot of time to finish. Many companies are embracing Hadoop for advanced data analytics over large datasets that require completion-time guarantees. Efficiency, especially the I/O costs of MapReduce, still need to be addressed for successful implications.

In this chapter, we will discuss some optimization techniques such as using compression and using Combiners in order to improve job execution. Also in this chapter, you will learn basic guidelines and rules to optimize your mappers and reducers code, and techniques to use and reuse the object's instances.

The following topics will be covered in this chapter:

- The benefits of using Combiners
- The importance of using compression
- Learning to use appropriate Writable types
- How to reuse types smartly
- How to optimize your mappers and reducers' code

Using Combiners

You can improve your overall MapReduce performance using **Combiners**. A Combiner is equivalent to a local Reduce operation and can effectively improve the rate of subsequent global Reduce operations. Basically, it is used to preliminarily optimize and minimize the number of key/value pairs that will be transmitted across the network between mappers and reducers. A Combiner will process the intermediate results of the key/value pairs' output using Map operations and it does not impact the transformation logic coded in the `map` and `reduce` functions.

The standard convention using Combiners is just to repurpose your reducer function as your Combiner. The computing logic should be **Commutative** (the order in which an operation such as addition is processed has no effect on the final result) and **Associative** (the order in which we apply the addition operation has no effect on the final result).

To get more information about Commutative and Associative properties, you can browse the following links:

http://en.wikipedia.org/wiki/Commutative_property
http://en.wikipedia.org/wiki/Associative_property

Implementing a Combiner means to implement a Combiner class. Once the customized class is implemented and added, the Map function will not immediately write to the output to produce intermediate results of key/value pairs. Instead, they will be collected to lists, and each key corresponds to a list of values. The Combiner class will output the key and corresponding value list in the form of key/value pairs. When the Combiner buffer reaches a certain number of key/value pairs, the data in the buffer is cleared and transferred to the Reduce function.

Calling your Combiner customized class for a job is similar to how the map and reduce classes are set:

```
job.setCombinerClass(MyCombine.class);
```

The following screenshot shows the Hadoop counters you should focus on when using Combiners:

	Counter	Map	Reduce	Total
Map-Reduce Framework	Map input bytes	1,048,576,000	0	1,048,576,000
	SPLIT_RAW_BYTES	1,504	0	1,504
	Combine input records	0	0	0
	Reduce input records	0	10,485,760	10,485,760
	Reduce input groups	0	10,485,760	10,485,760
	Combine output records	0	0	0
	Physical memory (bytes) snapshot	4,094,578,688	912,048,128	5,006,626,816
	Reduce output records	0	10,485,760	10,485,760
	Virtual memory (bytes) snapshot	18,717,839,360	3,535,028,224	22,252,867,584
	Map output records	10,485,760	0	10,485,760

In this screenshot, you can observe the number of records of **Combine input records** and **Combine output records,** which is **0** because the job doesn't implement any Combiner class. Therefore, the number of **Reduce input records** is the same as **Map output records**. The following screenshot shows the Combiner's effect once it has been implemented:

	Counter	Map	Reduce	Total
Map-Reduce Framework	Map input bytes	1,048,576,000	0	1,048,576,000
	SPLIT_RAW_BYTES	1,504	0	1,504
	Combine input records	10,485,760	0	10,485,760
	Reduce input records	0	685,760	685,760
	Reduce input groups	0	10,485,760	10,485,760
	Combine output records	685,760	0	685,760
	Physical memory (bytes) snapshot	4,094,578,688	912,048,128	5,006,626,816
	Reduce output records	0	485,760	485,760
	Virtual memory (bytes) snapshot	18,717,839,360	3,535,028,224	22,252,867,584
	Map output records	10,485,760	0	10,485,760

In this screenshot, notice the number of records of **Combine input records, Combine output records**, and the number of **Reduce input records** and **Map output records**. You will observe that implementing the Combiner reduced the data volume transferred to the Reduce function.

Comparing to the previous figure, the number of Combine records for this job has increased due to the use of the Combiner function. The Reduce input data volume has been dropped to **685,760** while it was initially **10,485,760**. In a very large data context, using Combiners is an efficient way to improve the MapReduce job's overall performance.

The following snippet of code illustrates a custom Combiner class extracted from a MapReduce job:

```
1   // Custom Combiner class sample
2   public static class Combine implements Reducer<Text, Text, Text, Text> {
3
4       //Like a reducer function, the combiner
5       //will be called with multiple values
6       //of map outputs
7       @Override
8       public void reduce(Text key, Iterator<Text> values, OutputCollector<Text,
9       Text> output, Reporter reporter) throws IOException {
10          Text prevTxt = null;
11
12          while (values.hasNext()) {
13              Text txt = values.next();
14
15              //output a key/value pair
16              //only if it is a new value.
17              if (!txt.equals(prevTxt)) {
18                  output.collect(key, txt);
19              }
20
21              //Cloning the iterator value objects supplied
22              //to the combiner to avoid values override
23              prevTtxt = ReflectionUtils.copy(job, txt, prevTxt);
24          }
25      }
26  }
```

As you can see, the `Combine` class implements the `Reducer` interface, and like a reducer function, it will be called with multiple values of the map output. This class overrides the `reduce()` method with its own code. The sample code between lines 12 and 23 iterates over the list of values transmitted by the `mapper` function and if the current key is different from the previous key, it calls the `collect()` method to output the result.

Using compression

Compression reduces the number of bytes read from or written to the underlying storage system (HDFS). Compression enhances efficiency of network bandwidth and disk space. Using data compression is important in Hadoop especially in a very large data context and under intensive workloads. In such a context, I/O operations and network data transfers take a considerable amount of time to complete. Moreover, the Shuffle and Merge process will also be under huge I/O pressure.

Because disk I/O and network bandwidth are precious resources in Hadoop, data compression is helpful to save these resources and minimize I/O disk and network transfer. Achieving increased performance and saving these resources is not free, although it is done with low CPU costs while compressing and decompressing operations.

Whenever I/O disk or network traffic affects your MapReduce job performance, you can improve the end-to-end processing time and reduce I/O and network traffic by enabling compression during any of the MapReduce phases.

 Compressing the map outputs will always contribute in reducing the network traffic between map and reduce tasks.

Compression may be enabled during any phase of the MapReduce job, as shown in the following figure:

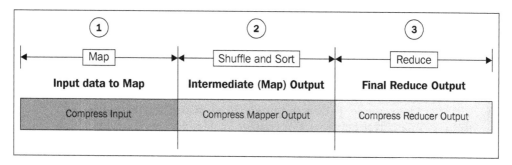

- **Compress Input**: This should be considered in a very large data context that you plan to process repeatedly. Therefore, you do not need to explicitly specify a codec to use. Hadoop will automatically check for the extension of your files and if it detects an appropriate extension, it will use the appropriate codec to compress and decompress your files. Otherwise, no compression codec will be used by Hadoop.

 When using replication, compressing input files saves storage space and speeds up data transfer. To compress input data, you should use splittable algorithms such as bzip2, or use zlib with the SequenceFile format.

- **Compress Mapper output**: Compression should be considered at this stage if your map tasks output a large amount of intermediate data. This will significantly improve the internal shuffle process, which is the most resource-consuming Hadoop process. You should always consider using compression if you observe slow network transfers due to large data volumes. To compress Mapper outputs, use faster codecs such as LZO, LZ4, or Snappy.

> **Limpel-Zif-Oberhumer (LZO)** is a common compression codec used in Hadoop to compress data. It was designed to keep up with the hard disk reading speed and therefore consider speed as priority, not compression rate. In comparison to the **gzip** codec, it compresses about five times faster and decompresses two times faster. A compressed file with LZO is 50 percent larger than the same file compressed with gzip, but still 25-50 percent smaller than the original file size, which is good to enhance performance and the map phase completes about four times faster.

- **Compress Reducer output**: Enabling compression at this stage will reduce the amount of data to be stored and therefore the required disk space. This is also useful if you chain MapReduce jobs together while the input files of the second job are already compressed.

> Compressing Reducer output should be considered for storage and/ or archival, better write speeds, or MapReduce jobs. To compress Reducer output, use standard utilities such as gzip or bzip2 for data interchange, and faster codecs for chained jobs.

The following screenshot shows the number of bytes written and read by a MapReduce job before enabling compression on map's output files:

	Counter	Map	Reduce	Total
	FILE_BYTES_READ	0	858	858
	HDFS_BYTES_READ	2,684,356,900	0	2,684,356,900
FileSystemCounters	FILE_BYTES_WRITTEN	565,862	57,237	623,099
	HDFS_BYTES_WRITTEN	0	80	80

In order to enable map output file compression, you can change these configuration parameters (in the mapred-site.xml file) as follows:

```
<property>
<name>mapred.compress.map.output</name>
<value>true</value>
</property>

<property>
<name>mapred.output.compression.type</name>
<value>BLOCK</value>
</property>
```

By default, the `mapred.compress.map.output` value is set to `false`, and the `mapred.output.compression.type` value is set to RECORD. Changing this value to BLOCK enhances compression ratio.

After enabling compression for the map output files, the number of bytes read by the reduce function (**268**) has considerably decreased in comparison to the previous figure (**858**), as illustrated in the following figure:

	Counter	Map	Reduce	Total
	FILE_BYTES_READ	0	268	268
	HDFS_BYTES_READ	2,684,356,900	0	2,684,356,900
FileSystemCounters	FILE_BYTES_WRITTEN	565,850	56,645	622,495
	HDFS_BYTES_WRITTEN	0	79	79

In order to enable compression in Hadoop, you can set the configuration parameters as shown in the following table:

Parameter	Default value	Stage	Recommendations
`io.compression.codec`	DefaultCodec	Input compress	Hadoop uses file extensions to determine whether a compression codec is supported
`mapreduce.map.output.compress`	false	Mapper output	Set this parameter to `true` to enable compression
`mapreduce.map.output.compress.codec`	DefaultCodec	Mapper output	Use LZO, LZ4 or Snappy codec to compress data at this stage
`mapreduce.output.fileoutputformat.compress`	false	Reducer output	Set this parameter to `true` to enable compression

Parameter	Default value	Stage	Recommendations

`mapreduce.output.`
`fileoutputformat.`
`compress.codec`
	`DefaultCodec`	Reducer
		output
			Use standard tool/codec
			such as `gzip` or `bzip2`

`mapreduce.output.`
`fileoutputformat.`
`compress.type`
	`RECORD`	Reducer
		output
			Type of compression
			to use for SequenceFile
			outputs: `NONE` and `BLOCK`

Using appropriate Writable types

Hadoop uses custom datatype serialization/RPC mechanism and defines its own *box* type classes. These classes are used to manipulate strings (`Text`), integers (`IntWritable`), and so on, and they implement the `Writable` class, which defines a deserialization protocol.

Therefore, all `values` in Hadoop are `Writable` type objects and all `keys` are instances of `WritableComparable`, which defines a sort order, because they need to be compared.

Writable objects are mutable and considerably more compact as no meta info needs to be stored (class name, fields, super classes, and so on), and straightforward random access gives higher performance. As binary `Writable` types will take up less space, this will reduce the size of intermediate data written by the Map or Combiner function. Reducing intermediate data can provide a substantial performance gain by reducing network transfer and I/O disk required storage space.

Using the appropriate Writable type in your code will contribute to enhancing the overall MapReduce job performance. This is mostly done by eliminating time for string splitting by using the `Text` type instead of the `String` type. Also, using `VIntWritable` or `VLongWritable` can sometimes be faster to use than regular `int` and `long` primitive Java datatypes.

During the Shuffle and Sort phase, comparing intermediate keys may be a bottleneck and Hadoop may spend time in this phase. Implementing a new comparison mechanism can improve your MapReduce performance. There are two ways to compare your keys:

- By implementing the `org.apache.hadoop.io.WritableComparable` interface
- By implementing the `RawComparator` interface

Based on our experience, implementing raw byte comparisons using `RawComparator` improves the overall performance of the MapReduce job and has an advantage over `WritableComparable`.

A typical implementation of `WritableComparable` class will look like the following snippet of code:

```
1  public class MyClass implements WritableComparable<MyClass> {
2      private IntWritable i;
3      private IntWritable j;
4      //....
5  }
```

To implement `RawComparator`, you can also extend the `WritableComparator` class, which implements `RawComparator`. The following snippet of code illustrates a typical implementation of the `WritableComparator` class:

```
1  public class MyClassComparator extends WritableComparator {
2      protected MyClassComparator() {
3          super(MyClass.class);
4      }
5
6      @Override
7      public int compare(byte[] b1, int s1, int l1, byte[] b2, int s2, int l2) {
8          int i1 = readInt(b1, s1);
9          int i2 = readInt(b2, s2);
10         //....
11
12     }
13 }
```

Extending the `WritableComparator` class allows you to use inherited methods of this class to manipulate your intermediate MapReduce keys.

The `readInt()` method inherited from `WritableComparator` converts 4 consecutive bytes into a primitive Java `int` (which is 4 bytes).

To wire up your `RawComparator` custom class implementation, set its sort comparator class as follows:

```
job.setSortComparatorClass(MyClassComparator.class);
```

Depending on the data you want to process, you may need to define how to read your data file into the Mappers instances. Hadoop allows you to define your own data format by implementing the InputFormat interface and comes with several implementations of it.

> The InputFormat class is one of the fundamental classes of the Hadoop framework, and it is responsible for defining two main things: InputSplit and RecordReader.

An InputFormat class describes both how to present the data to the Mapper and where the data originates from. The InputSplit interface defines both the size of individual map tasks and its execution server. The RecordReader interface is responsible for reading records from the input file, and submitting them (as key/value pairs) to the mappers. Another important job of the InputFormat class is to split the input files sources into fragments, represented by FileInputSplit instances. These fragments are used as the input for individual mappers. In order to improve the job's performance, this process must be quick enough and cheap (it should use minimum CPU, I/O storage, and network resources).

> When creating your own InputFormat class, it is better to subclass the FileInputFormat class rather than to implement InputFormat directly.

Reusing types smartly

Often, Hadoop problems are caused by some form of memory mismanagement and nodes don't suddenly fail but experience slowdown as I/O devices go bad. Hadoop has many options for controlling memory allocation and usage at several levels of granularity, but it does not check these options. So, it is possible for the combined heap size for all the daemons on a machine to exceed the amount of physical memory.

Each Java process itself has a configured maximum heap size. Depending on whether the JVM heap size, OS limit, or physical memory is exhausted first, this will cause an out-of-memory error, a JVM abort, or severe swapping, respectively.

You should pay attention to memory management. All unnecessarily allocated memory resources should be removed to maximize memory space for the MapReduce jobs.

Reusing types is a technique for minimizing resources usage such as CPU and memory space. When you deal with millions of data records, it is always cheaper to reuse an existing instance rather than create a new one. The simplest kind of reusability in a MapReduce job is to use an existing Hadoop Writable type as it is, and this is possible in most circumstances.

One of the most common error with beginners when coding a `map` or `reduce` function is to allocate a new object for every output and often this is done inside a `for` or `foreach` loop, which may create thousands or millions of new `Writable` instances. These instances have very short **TTL (Time To Live)** and enforce Java's garbage collector to have an intensive job to deal with all allocated memory required by them.

The following snippet of code shows a mapper function that allocates a new `Writable` instance for every output (you should avoid coding this way).

```
1  public void MyMapper extends MapReduceBase implements Mapper {
2      ...
3      for (String word : words) {
4          output.collect(new Text(word), new IntWritable(1));
5      }
6  }
```

In order to detect whether you are spending time on allocating resources for unnecessary objects, you should inspect your tasks' logs and analyze the garbage collector activities. If it represents a lot of time and is frequent, it means you should review your code and enhance it by eliminating the unnecessary creation of new objects.

This is because if you have low memory, creating new objects will be stored in heap memory as long as a certain memory threshold is exceeded and the garbage collector must run more often.

 Reusing Writable variables is theoretically better, but based on Amdahl's law (`http://en.wikipedia.org/wiki/Amdahl%27s_law`), the improvement may not be noticeable.

Logs are commonly used to diagnose issues. Often, the line that indicates the problem is buried in thousands of lines. Picking out the relevant line is a long and fastidious task. To inspect MapReduce tasks logs in more detail, you should set the JVM memory parameters in the `mapred-site.xml` configuration file, as shown in the following table:

Parameter	Default value	Recommendations
`mapred.child.java.opts`	`-Xmx200m`	Add: `-verbose:gc` `-XX:+PrintGCDetails`

The following snippet of code shows a better way to find the benefits of reusing `Writable` variables:

```
1   public void MyMapper extends MapReduceBase implements Mapper {
2       ...
3       Text text = new Text();
4       IntWritable i = new IntWritable(1);
5       ...
6       for (String word : words) {
7           text.set(word);
8           output.collect(word, i);
9       }
10  }
```

JVM reuse is an optimization technique of reusing JVMs for multiple tasks. If it is enabled, multiple tasks can be executed sequentially with one JVM. You can enable JVM reuse by changing the appropriate parameter in the `mapred-site.xml` configuration file as shown in the following table:

Parameter	Default value	Recommendations
`mapred.job.reuse.jvm.num.tasks`	1	Change this variable to run the desired number of tasks (for example, 2 to run two tasks). If this variable is set to `-1`, the number of tasks the JVM can execute is not limited.

Optimizing mappers and reducers code

Optimizing MapReduce code-side performance in detail exceeds the scope of this book. In this section, we will provide a basic guideline with some rules to contribute to the improvement of your MapReduce job performance.

One of the important features of Hadoop is that all data is processed in a unit known as **records**. While records have almost the same size, theoretically, the time to process such records should be the same. However, in practice, the processing time of records within a task vary significantly and slowness may appear when reading a record from memory, processing the record, or writing the record to memory. Moreover, in practice, two other factors may affect the mapper or reducer performance: I/O access time and spill, and overhead waiting time resulting from heavy I/O requests.

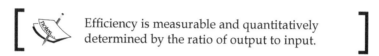 Efficiency is measurable and quantitatively determined by the ratio of output to input.

MapReduce provides ease of use while a programmer defines his job with only Map and Reduce functions, without having to specify physical distribution of his job across nodes. Therefore, Hadoop provides a fixed dataflow to perform a MapReduce job. This is why many complex algorithms are hard to implement with mapper(s) and reducer(s) only in a MapReduce job. In addition, some algorithms that require multiple inputs are not well supported since the dataflow of MapReduce is originally designed to read a single input and generate a single output.

Optimizing a MapReduce job means:

- Getting the same output in less time
- Using less resources to get the same output and in the same time
- Getting more output with same resources in the same time

In any programming language, factorizing your code is the first optimization step. If you run multiple jobs to process the same input data, it is probably the opportunity to rewrite them into fewer jobs. Also, when writing your mapper or reducer function code, you should choose the most efficient underlying algorithm, which will contribute to speeding up your job, otherwise you may have to deal with slowness and/or bad performance. Therefore, inefficiencies in your code can slow down your MapReduce jobs.

Check the current logging level of JobTracker with the following command:

```
hadoop daemonlog -getlevel {HadoopMachineName}:50030 org.
apache.hadoop.mapred.JobTracker
```

Set the Hadoop log debug level for JobTracker as follows:

```
hadoop daemonlog -setlevel {HadoopMachineName}:50030 org.
apache.hadoop.mapred.JobTracker DEBUG
```

The second step is to determine whether there is a problem when executing your MapReduce job. All mappers/reducers should terminate successfully when they see that the number of failed tasks on this job is zero. If this number is nonzero, basically there is something wrong with your program. If the number is low (two or three) the node may be unstable.

Sometimes it's not just your job that caused the problem, but something else might be causing the problem.

Some algorithms require global state information during their processing, while MapReduce does not treat state information during its execution. MapReduce reads data iteratively and materializes intermediate results on local disk in each iteration, which require lot of I/O operations. If you need to implement such algorithms, you should consider using third-party tools such as HaLoop (http://code.google.com/p/haloop/) or Twister (http://www.iterativemapreduce.org/).

You can enhance your MapReduce job by reducing distribution time and network bandwidth required by Hadoop to distribute a heavy application. Remember that the MapReduce framework presumes a compute-light application, as the compute task needs to get transmitted across to each of the nodes of the cluster where it is scheduled to run in parallel. Transferring applications that have a very large code footprint across the nodes of the cluster would take so much time that it would completely drain the throughput benefit expected to be achieved from parallel execution of its multiple instances.

Try pre-installing your computation task on all nodes; it would completely avoid the need for task distribution and the associated time loss.

Remember that MapReduce is designed to process a very large data volume as an input record. If, for some reason, your mapper fails to read an input record, it would be counterproductive to kill the task each time it fails because at the end, the result will remain the same, a mapper task that still fails.

To prevent such a situation, you should handle input error in the reader and report this error (sometimes you need to create a custom OutputFormat class) so it can be tracked by an administrator or while debugging a session.

 If your application tolerates record skipping, Hadoop will provide you with a feature for skipping over records through the SkipBadRecords class:

```
setMapperMaxSkipRecords(Configuration conf,long
maxSkipRecs)

setReducerMaxSkipGroups(Configuration conf,long
maxSkipGrps)
```

Summary

In this chapter, we learned about MapReduce Combiners and how they help to improve the overall execution job time. Also, we covered why it is important to use compression, especially in a large data volume context.

Then we covered Java code-side optimization and learned about choosing appropriate Writable types and how to reuse these types smartly. We also learned about WritableComparator and RawComparator custom class implementation.

In the final section, we covered basic guidelines with some rules to tune your Hadoop configuration and enhance its performance.

In the next chapter, we will learn more about MapReduce optimization best practices. Keep reading!

7
Best Practices and Recommendations

Well, this is the grand finale! So far, we learned how to optimize MapReduce job performance and dedicated a major part of this book to laying down some important fundamentals. Remember that setting up a Hadoop cluster is basically the challenge of combining the requirements of high availability, load balancing, and the individual requirements of the services you aim to get from your cluster servers.

In this chapter, we will describe the hardware and application configuration checklists that you can use to optimize your Hadoop MapReduce jobs.

The following topics will be covered in this chapter:

- The common Hadoop cluster checklist
- The BIOS checklist and OS recommendations
- Hadoop best practices and recommendations
- A MapReduce template class to use in your application

Hardware tuning and OS recommendations

Recommendations for system tuning depend on the intrinsic capabilities of the system. The following sections suggest different recommendation techniques and tips that you can use as reminder baselines when engaging in your MapReduce optimization process.

The Hadoop cluster checklist

The following checklist describes only the minimal set of steps required to get your Hadoop cluster working optimally:

- Check and ensure that all cluster nodes can communicate with each other and you have physical and/or remote management access to each cluster node
- Check whether your cluster is well dimensioned and is able to compensate a failure of (at least) one node per service
- Check the limitations of your cluster environment (hardware availability resources/rack space, hosting parameters, and so on)
- Define your cluster strategies for a failover to ensure high availability of your services
- Define what you need to back up, and what needs to be saved and where, in order to maximize your Hadoop storage capacity

The Bios tuning checklist

This topic lists what you should check while installing Hadoop cluster nodes to be used in an optimal environment. The following checks are to be carried out:

- Check whether all CPU cores on the hardware are fully utilized; otherwise, you can downgrade the CPU frequency.
- Enable **Native Command Queuing mode (NCQ)**, which helps improve I/O performance of modern hard drives by optimizing the drive head's movement. Usually, the NCQ mode can be enabled through the **Advanced Host Controller Interface (AHCI)** option in BIOS.

Check whether there are any default BIOS settings that may negatively affect your Hadoop MapReduce jobs.

OS configuration recommendations

In this minimal checklist, we present some recommendations for system tuning, which are a combination of CPU, I/O, and memory techniques. The following are the recommendations:

- Choose a Linux distribution that supports the EXT4 filesystem.
- By default, every file's read operation triggers a disk write operation in order to maintain the time the file was last accessed. This extra disk activity associated with updating the access time is not desired. You can disable this logging of access time for both files and directories using `noatime` on the filesystem.

nodiratime: This disables updating of the access time when opening directories so that the access time is not modified when enumerating directories.

- Avoid using **Logical Volume Management** (**LVM**), which is used to manage disk drives and similar mass-storage devices as this will affect the disk's I/O performance.

- Set the Linux kernel's swap memory to a low value. This informs the Linux kernel that it should try to avoid swapping as much as possible.

- Linux kernels' I/O scheduling controls how input/output operations will be submitted to the storage. Experiment with the **Completely Fair Queuing** (**CFQ**) of the I/O scheduler, which is similar to the round-robin algorithm in the way that the I/O operations are implemented as a circular queue, and a fixed execution time is allowed for each I/O operation.

- Increase the Linux OS max open file descriptors, which may enhance the MapReduce job performance.

Hadoop best practices and recommendations

In order to improve Hadoop performance, these are some configuration tips and recommendations that represent compendium of best practices for applications running on the Hadoop framework.

Deploying Hadoop

Hadoop can be installed manually by downloading its archived files from the official website and copying it to the cluster. This will work, but it is not recommended if you want to install Hadoop on more than four node clusters. Installing Hadoop manually on a large cluster can lead to issues with maintenance and troubleshooting. Any configuration changes need to be applied manually to all nodes using **Secure Copy Protocol** (**SCP**) or **Secure Shell** (**SSH**).

To deploy Hadoop on a large cluster, it is recommended (and a good practice) to use a configuration management system and/or automated deployment tools such as Cloudera (http://www.cloudera.com), Hortonworks (http://hortonworks.com), and the MapR (http://www.mapr.com) management system. For additional work, such as application deployment, it is good to use Yum and Puppet.

You can use these tools to build and maintain Hadoop clusters for the following:

- Setup
- Configuration
- Scalability
- Monitoring
- Maintenance
- Troubleshooting

 Puppet is a powerful open source tool that helps you to perform administrative tasks such as adding users, installing packages, and updating server configurations based on a centralized specification. You can learn more about Puppet by browsing the following link: http://puppetlabs.com/puppet/what-is-puppet.

Hadoop tuning recommendations

The checklists and recommendations given in this section will be useful to prepare and follow MapReduce performance recommendations.

The following is the checklist for Memory recommendations:

- Adjust memory settings to avoid a job hanging due to insufficient memory
- Set or define a JVM reuse policy
- Verify the JVM code cache and increase it if necessary
- Analyze **garbage collector** (**GC**) cycles (using detailed logs), observe whether it has an intensive cycle (which means there is a large number of object instances created in memory) and check the Hadoop framework heap usage

The following are the massive I/O tuning recommendations to ensure that there are no setbacks due to I/O operations:

- In the context of large input data, compress source data to avoid/reduce massive I/O tuning
- Reduce spilled records from map tasks when you experiment with large spilled records

  Reduce spilled records by tuning: io.sort.mb, io.sort.record.percent, io.sort.spill.percent
- Compress the map output to minimize I/O disk operations

- Implement a Combiner to minimize massive I/O and network traffic

  Add a Combiner with the following line of code:

  job.setCombinerClass(Reduce.class);

- Compress the MapReduce job output to minimize large output data effects

  The compression parameters are `mapred.compress.map.output` and `mapred.output.compression.type`

- Change the replication parameter value to minimize network traffic and massive I/O disk operations

The Hadoop minimal configuration checklist to validate hardware resources is as follows:

- Define the Hadoop ecosystem components that are required to be installed (and maintained)

- Define how you are going to install Hadoop, manually or using an automated deployment tool (such as Puppet/Yum)

- Choose the underlying core storage such as HDFS, HBase, and so on

- Check whether additional components are required for orchestration, job scheduling, and so on

- Check on third-party software dependencies such as JVM version

- Check the key parameter configuration of Hadoop, such as HDFS block size, replication factor, and compression

- Define the monitoring policy; what should be monitored and with which tool (for example, Ganglia)

- Install a monitoring tool, such as Nagios or Ganglia, to monitor your Hadoop cluster resources

- Identify (calculate) the amount of required disk space to store the job data

- Identify (calculate) the number of required nodes to perform the job

- Check whether NameNodes and DataNodes have the required minimal hardware resources, such as amount of RAM, number of CPUs, and network bandwidth

- Calculate the number of mapper and reducer tasks required to maximize CPU usage

- Check the number of MapReduce tasks to ensure that sufficient tasks are running

- Avoid using the Virtual server for the production environment and use it only for your MapReduce application development

- Eliminate map-side spills and reduce-side disk I/O

Using a MapReduce template class code

Most MapReduce applications are similar to each other. Often, you can create one basic application template, customize the map() and reduce() functions, and reuse it.

The code snippet in the following screenshot shows you a MapReduce template class that you can enhance and customize to meet your needs:

```
1    import org.apache.hadoop.conf.Configuration;
2    import org.apache.hadoop.conf.Configured;
3    import org.apache.hadoop.fs.Path;
4    import org.apache.hadoop.io.LongWritable;
5    import org.apache.hadoop.io.RawComparator;
6    import org.apache.hadoop.io.Text;
7    import org.apache.hadoop.mapreduce.Job;
8    import org.apache.hadoop.mapreduce.Mapper;
9    import org.apache.hadoop.mapreduce.Partitioner;
10   import org.apache.hadoop.mapreduce.Reducer;
11   import org.apache.hadoop.mapreduce.lib.input.FileInputFormat;
12   import org.apache.hadoop.mapreduce.lib.output.FileOutputFormat;
13   import org.apache.hadoop.util.Tool;
14   import org.apache.hadoop.util.ToolRunner;
15
16   import java.io.IOException;
17
18   public class MapReduceTemplate extends Configured implements Tool {
19
```

In the preceding screenshot, lines 1-16 are declarations for all Java classes that will be used in the application.

In the preceding screenshot, in line 18 the MapReduceTemplate class is a declaration. This class extends the Configured class and implements the Tool interface. The following screenshot represents the mapper function:

```
19
20          public static class Map extends
21                  Mapper<LongWritable, Text, LongWritable, Text> {
22              @Override
23              protected void map(LongWritable key, Text values, Context context)
24                      throws IOException, InterruptedException {
25              // your map code goes here
26
27              /* do not forget to catch exceptions
28                  try {
29
30                      } catch (NumberFormatException e) {
31                          // cannot parse - ignore
32                      }
33              */
34              }
35
36          }
37
```

In the preceding screenshot, from lines 20-36, the `static class Map` definition
represents your mapper function, as shown in the previous screenshot. This class
extends the `Mapper` class and the `map()` function should be overridden by your
code. It is recommended that you catch any exception to prevent the failure of a map
task without terminating its process. The code snippets in the following screenshot
represent the static class Reduce definition:

```
37
38          public static class Reduce extends
39                  Reducer<LongWritable, Text, LongWritable, Text> {
40              @Override
41              protected void reduce(LongWritable key, Iterable<Text> values,
42                      Context context) throws IOException, InterruptedException {
43              // your reduce function goes here
44
45              /* do not forget to catch exceptions
46                  try {
47
48                      } catch (NumberFormatException e) {
49                          // cannot parse - ignore
50                      }
51              */
52              }
53
54          }
55
```

In the preceding screenshot, from lines 38-54, the `static class Reduce` `definition` represents your `Reducer` function shown in the previous code screenshot. This class extends the Reducer class and the `reduce ()` function should be overridden by your code. It is recommended that you catch any exception to prevent the reduce task from failing before terminating its process:

```
public static class P extends Partitioner<Text, LongWritable> {
    @Override
    public int getPartition(Text key, LongWritable value, int parts) {
        // your partitioner function code goes here
        // Partitioner function example

        int hash = key.toString().hashCode();
        return (hash & Integer.MAX_VALUE) % parts;
    }
}

public static class G implements RawComparator<Text> {
    public int compare(Text o1, Text o2) {
        return 0;
    }

    public int compare(byte[] b1, int s1, int l1, byte[] b2, int s2, int l2) {
        return 0;
    }
}

public static class C implements RawComparator<Text> {
    public int compare(Text o1, Text o2) {
        return 0;
    }

    public int compare(byte[] b1, int s1, int l1, byte[] b2, int s2, int l2) {
        return 0;
    }
}
```

In the preceding screenshot, from lines 56-85, the different class implementations are optional. These classes will help you to define a custom key practitioner, group, and sort class comparators, as mentioned in the previous screenshot. The run() method implementation is shown in the following screenshot:

```
86
87   public int run(String[] args) throws Exception {
88       Job job = new Job(getConf(), "This is a MapReduceTemplate!");
89       job.setJarByClass(MapReduceTemplate.class);
90
91       job.setMapperClass(Map.class);
92       job.setCombinerClass(Reduce.class);
93       job.setReducerClass(Reduce.class);
94
95       job.setPartitionerClass(P.class);
96       job.setGroupingComparatorClass(G.class);
97       job.setSortComparatorClass(C.class);
98
99       FileInputFormat.addInputPaths(job, args[0]);
100
101      // job.setInputFormatClass(LzoTextInputFormat.class);
102      // LzoTextInputFormat.addInputPaths(job, args[0]);
103
104      job.setOutputKeyClass(LongWritable.class);
105      job.setOutputValueClass(Text.class);
106      FileOutputFormat.setOutputPath(job, new Path(args[1]));
107
108      // job.setOutputFormatClass(TextOutputFormat.class);
109      // TextOutputFormat.setOutputPath(job, new Path(args[1]));
110      // TextOutputFormat.setCompressOutput(job, true);
111      // TextOutputFormat.setOutputCompressorClass(job, GzipCodec.class);
112
113      // job.setOutputFormatClass(SequenceFileOutputFormat.class);
114      // SequenceFileOutputFormat.setOutputPath(job, new Path(args[1]));
115      // SequenceFileOutputFormat.setCompressOutput(job, true);
116      // SequenceFileOutputFormat.setOutputCompressorClass(job,
117      // GzipCodec.class);
118      // SequenceFileOutputFormat.setOutputCompressionType(job,
119      // CompressionType.BLOCK);
120
121      boolean successful = job.waitForCompletion(true);
122
123      System.out.println(job.getJobID()
124          + (successful ? " :successful" : " :failed"));
125
126      return successful ? 0 : 1;
127  }
128
```

In the preceding screenshot, from lines 87-127 comprise the `run()` method implementation. The MapReduce job is configured and its parameters are set within this method, such as the Map and Reduce class, as shown in the previous screenshot. You can now enable compression, set the `OutputKey` class, the `FileOutputFormat` class, and so on. The code in the following screenshot represents the `main()` method:

```
128
129      /**
130       * @param args
131       * @throws Exception
132       */
133      public static void main(String[] args) throws Exception {
134          System.out.println("Running MapReduceTemplate job!");
135          System.exit(ToolRunner.run(new Configuration(), new MapReduceTemplate(), args));
136      }
137
138  }
139
```

In the preceding screenshot, from lines 133-138, the `main()` method implementation is specified. Within this method, a new configuration instance is created and the `run()` method is called to launch the MapReduce job.

Some other factors to consider when writing your application are as follows:

- When you have large output file (multiple GBs), consider using a larger output block size by setting `dfs.block.size`.

- To improve HDFS write performance, choose an appropriate compressor codec (compression speed versus efficiency) to compress the application's output.

- Avoid writing out more than one output file per reduce.

- Use an appropriate file format for the output of the reducers.

- Use only splittable compression codec to write out a large amount of compressed textual data. Codec such as `zlib/gzip/lzo` is counter-productive because it cannot be split and processed, which forces the MapReduce framework to process the entire file in a single map. Consider using `SequenceFile` file formats, since they are compressed and splittable.

Summary

In this chapter, we learned about the best practices of Hadoop MapReduce optimization. In order to improve the job performance of Hadoop, several recommendations and tips were presented in the form of checklists, which will help you to ensure that your Hadoop cluster is well configured and dimensioned.

This concludes our journey of learning to optimize and enhance our MapReduce job performance. I hope you have enjoyed it as much as I did. I encourage you to keep learning more about the topics covered in this book using the MapReduce published papers on Google, Hadoop's official website, and other sources on the Internet. Optimizing a MapReduce job is an iterative and repeatable process that you need to do before finding out its optimum performance. Also, I recommend that you try different techniques to figure out which tuning solutions are most efficient in the context of your job and try combining different optimization techniques!

Index

performance tuning
  categories 32
  components 15
  diagram 33
  goal 32
  of Hadoop MapReduce job 32
  steps 32
pseudo formula 52

R

rack awareness concept 21
RAM bottlenecks
  identifying 37
readInt() method 79
read-only default configuration 16
Read phase 56
Record length (RL) 61
records 83
reduce () function 94
reduce function 9
Reduce phase
  enhancing, parameters 66
Reducer function 94
reducers code
  optimizing 83, 85
Reduce tasks
  enhancing 63-65
  phases 63
  Reduce phase 64
  Shuffle phase 64
  Write phase 64
Reduce tasks, enhancing
  map parameters, tuning 67-69
  Reduce execution phase, improving 65, 66
  reduce parameters, tuning 67-69
  Reduce phase 64
  reduce task throughput, calculating 64, 65
  Shuffle phase, profiling 64
  Write phase, profiling 64
reduce tasks(reducers) 11
resource bottlenecks
  CPU bottlenecks, identifying 37, 38
  identifying 36
  network bandwidth bottlenecks, identifying 39, 40
  RAM bottlenecks, identifying 37

storage bottlenecks, identifying 38, 39
run() method 95, 96

S

Secure Copy Protocol (SCP) 89
Secure Shell (SSH) 89
Shuffle phase 64
site-specific configuration 16
SkipBadRecords class 85
small files
  packing, alternatives 58
Spilled Records size (RS) 61
Spill phase 56
split file 58, 59
storage bottlenecks
  identifying 38, 39
system performance
  analyzing 39

T

TaskTracker 10
tasktrakker.http.threads parameter 60
TeraGen modules 33
TeraSort modules 33
TeraValidate modules 33
TestDFSIO benchmark tool
  output log 39
  using 38
topology.script.file.name (core-site.xml)
        variable 21
TTL (Time to Live) 81
Twister 84
types
  reusing 81, 82

V

vmstat tool 47

W

Writable class 78
WritableComparable class 79
WritableComparator class 79
Writable type object
  writing 78, 80

Thank you for buying
Optimizing Hadoop for MapReduce

About Packt Publishing

Packt, pronounced 'packed', published its first book "*Mastering phpMyAdmin for Effective MySQL Management*" in April 2004 and subsequently continued to specialize in publishing highly focused books on specific technologies and solutions.

Our books and publications share the experiences of your fellow IT professionals in adapting and customizing today's systems, applications, and frameworks. Our solution based books give you the knowledge and power to customize the software and technologies you're using to get the job done. Packt books are more specific and less general than the IT books you have seen in the past. Our unique business model allows us to bring you more focused information, giving you more of what you need to know, and less of what you don't.

Packt is a modern, yet unique publishing company, which focuses on producing quality, cutting-edge books for communities of developers, administrators, and newbies alike. For more information, please visit our website: www.packtpub.com.

About Packt Open Source

In 2010, Packt launched two new brands, Packt Open Source and Packt Enterprise, in order to continue its focus on specialization. This book is part of the Packt Open Source brand, home to books published on software built around Open Source licenses, and offering information to anybody from advanced developers to budding web designers. The Open Source brand also runs Packt's Open Source Royalty Scheme, by which Packt gives a royalty to each Open Source project about whose software a book is sold.

Writing for Packt

We welcome all inquiries from people who are interested in authoring. Book proposals should be sent to author@packtpub.com. If your book idea is still at an early stage and you would like to discuss it first before writing a formal book proposal, contact us; one of our commissioning editors will get in touch with you.

We're not just looking for published authors; if you have strong technical skills but no writing experience, our experienced editors can help you develop a writing career, or simply get some additional reward for your expertise.

Hadoop MapReduce Cookbook

ISBN: 978-1-84951-728-7   Paperback: 300 pages

Recipes for analyzing large and complex datasets with Hadoop MapReduce

1. Learn to process large and complex data sets, starting simply, then diving in deep.

2. Solve complex big data problems such as classifications, finding relationships, online marketing, and recommendations.

3. More than 50 Hadoop MapReduce recipes, presented in a simple and straightforward manner, with step-by-step instructions and real world examples.

Instant MapReduce Patterns – Hadoop Essentials How-to

ISBN: 978-1-78216-770-9   Paperback: 60 pages

Practical recipes to write your own MapReduce solution patterns for Hadoop programs

1. Learn something new in an Instant! A short, fast, focused guide delivering immediate results.

2. Learn how to install, configure, and run Hadoop jobs.

3. Seven recipes, each describing a particular style of the MapReduce program to give you a good understanding of how to program with MapReduce.

Please check **www.PacktPub.com** for information on our titles

Hadoop Real-World Solutions Cookbook

ISBN: 978-1-84951-912-0   Paperback: 316 pages

Realistic, simple code examples to solve problems at scale with Hadoop and related technologies

1. Solutions to common problems when working in the Hadoop environment.

2. Recipes for (un)loading data, analytics, and troubleshooting.

3. In depth code examples demonstrating various analytic models, analytic solutions, and common best practices.

Big Data Analytics with R and Hadoop

ISBN: 978-1-78216-328-2   Paperback: 238 pages

Set up an integrated infrastructure of R and Hadoop to turn your data analytics into Big Data analytics

1. Write Hadoop MapReduce within R.

2. Learn data analytics with R and the Hadoop platform.

3. Handle HDFS data within R.

4. Understand Hadoop streaming with R.

5. Encode and enrich datasets into R.

Please check **www.PacktPub.com** for information on our titles